Understanding Business

Marketing Decisions

Peter Tinniswood

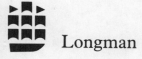
Longman

Longman Group UK Limited
Longman House
Burnt Mill, Harlow,
Essex CM20 2JE, England

First published 1981
Sixth Impression 1987

ISBN 0 582 35543 5

Produced by Longman Group (FE) Ltd
Printed in Hong Kong

Contents

Introduction to the Series

This series produces a new approach to the teaching of business. It is suitable for young managers, students and academic sixth-formers. It has been developed over the last decade to give understanding of the nature and purpose of business activity, whilst also stimulating the minds of the more academically gifted members of society.

The material provides for an analytical understanding of people's problems and behaviour within organisations. The texts discuss the nature of problems, and explore concepts and principles which may be employed to aid their solution. Test materials have been selected from industrial and commercial organisations; from the private and public sector; from non-profit-making institutions. The material is as much to provide general understanding about industrial society and the workings of organisations, as it is to help those who are already engaged in their business or professional career.

The approach of decision-making has been used to draw together ideas, and produce significant elements of reality; the approach gives purpose and challenge to the reader. Any organisation is striving towards more or less closely defined objectives by deciding how to carry out, and control, its activities within constantly changing conditions. The programme looks carefully at these processes of decision-making; it provides the student with an understanding of their overall nature. Ideas from the four functional areas of human behaviour, quantitative data, accounting and the economic environment are drawn together within a decision-making framework; the approach is then applied to different areas of business activity, particularly to those of finance, marketing and production.

This series of eight books has been designed to meet the needs of students (and their lecturers/teachers) studying the business world. The up-to-date materials within each book provide many ideas and activities from which the teacher can choose. Lecturers on management courses may use the book to introduce analytical concepts to practitioners; tertiary management courses may use them as a first text and as a source of well-tried and up-to-date cases; BEC and 'A' Level students may use the books as complete courses.

To meet these different needs, each book in the series has been designed to stand either as a part of the whole, or complete in its own right.

All books have the same chapter format:

a chapter objective and synopsis so that the purpose and pattern are clear;
a factual/explanatory text with case examples where applicable;
a participative work section to provide materials for learning, application and discussion.

The participative sections are an integral part of the whole text and allow students to gain understanding by doing. They are usually divided into three parts. Firstly, some simple revision questions to enable the students to check their own basic understanding. Secondly, a series of exercises and case problems to test their application and to increase their knowledge of the area. Thirdly, a set of essay questions.

There is a teachers' booklet accompanying each student text which introduces the topic area, clarifies possible objectives, suggests approaches to the selected materials and adds additional ideas. The teachers' booklets also provide solutions, where appropriate, to the participative work sections.

The philosophy, approach and materials have been forged in discussion with businessmen, lecturers and teachers. Trial and error has refined much of the text and most of the participative work. The whole venture has been co-ordinated by the Cambridge Business Studies Project Trust. Initial work developed from a link between the Wolfson Foundation, Marlborough College and Shell International Ltd. Trustees for the Project include Professor John Dancy, Sir Michael Clapham and Sir Nicholas Goodison; much early guidance was also given by Professor Sir Austin Robinson.

The series can be used as the basis for an 'A' Level examination run by the Cambridge Local Examinations Syndicate and established in 1967. The examination syllabus and objectives are in line with the materials in these texts.

Richard Barker
Series Editor

Author's Preface

Too often we hear of projects designed in one country and left to others to develop, of lost or unexploited markets as a result of apathy towards marketing, of opportunities missed through failure to match production with market requirements. The frontiers of technology are advancing rapidly but developments in that field have little value unless they are marketed. Without an aggressive marketing strategy the benefits of technology are lost both to manufacturer and consumer.

This book is an introduction to one of the most exciting aspects of business. Marketing is the interface between the consumer and the firm. It ranges from decisions on production policy to ways of creating a market and fulfilling a need. The essence of marketing lies in practical experience, but a clear grasp of the basic principles gives direction to the marketing effort and reduces the risk of wasted resources.

Case studies play a vital part in the understanding of marketing because they create practical situations and present problems for analysis. The book contains both imaginary and real case material, designed to illustrate the ideas of each chapter and provide the opportunity to apply the theory. The last chapter looks at four complete case situations to enable the student to bring together all the ideas in marketing.

Although the text uses masculine terms (he/man, etc), marketing is by no means the preserve of the male. Indeed, it is an area where women have been extremely successful. I have used the masculine merely for consistency and to avoid the interruptions of the 'he/she' format.

I should like to thank the students and teachers who have used the draft chapters and whose comments have been very valuable. Particularly, thanks to Jim Jamison who taught the area with me, and to John Powell for his comments on the numerate aspects.

The Advertising and Sales Policy and Sales Promotion chapters were kindly read by James Goble, Director of J. Walter Thompson; Richard Venables, Chairman of Ogilvey Benson and Mather; and also Richard Awdry, Director of Bell Chesney Malleson whose sense of humour was a great support throughout the book. These three gave freely of their valuable time, and their comments and suggestions have been an enormous help.

Author's Preface

I owe a debt of gratitude to my parents who read the manuscript and undertook the tiresome, but essential, job of proof reading.

Special thanks to Elizabeth Rhea for her competence and determination in typing the manuscript from my illegible scrawl.

Richard Barker always plays an important part in the production of any book in this series. His prodding, advice, encouragement and help throughout its stages have been invaluable.

Lastly, my thanks to the many people, too numerous to mention, who have provided information and ideas. Needless to say, such errors as remain are my own.

Peter Tinniswood
Marlborough College

Chapter 1

Introduction to Marketing

Objective: *To show why marketing has become important. To show how business organisations have come to depend on marketing and to show its all-embracing nature. To define the term 'marketing'.*

Synopsis: *The term 'marketing' is used in many ways, but all reflect some link between producer and consumer and establish it as a function in the business context. It radically influences the philosophy of the firm and its basic direction, as well as having a significant impact on the success of the organisation. Some organisations are market-orientated, determining their product range on the satisfaction of their customers, both existing and potential. Others are production-orientated. Their prime concern and expertise lie with what they are making. Selling is of secondary importance. The best mix of product and market-orientation is achieved through examination of the market and the nature of the product – some organisations need to be more market-orientated than others. However, mass production and competition have ensured that marketing plays an increasingly important role.*

Plan of the chapter:

- **1**.1 What is Marketing?
- **1**.2 The Change from Product to Market-Orientation
- **1**.3 The Importance and Need for Marketing
- **1**.4 Marketing: Summary and Definition

1.1 **What is Marketing?**

'Would you tell me, please, which way I ought to go from here?'
'That depends a good deal on where you want to get to,' said the Cat.
'I don't much care where ——' said Alice.
'Then it doesn't matter which way you go,' said the Cat.
'—— so long as I get *somewhere*,' Alice added as an explanation.
'Oh, you're sure to do that,' said the Cat, 'if you only walk long enough.'
Alice felt that this could not be denied, so she tried another question.

'What sort of people live about here?'

'In *that* direction,' the Cat said, waving its right paw round, 'lives a Hatter: and in *that* direction,' waving the other paw, 'lives a March Hare. Visit either you like: they're both mad.'

'But I don't want to go among mad people,' Alice remarked.

'Oh, you can't help that,' said the Cat: 'we're all mad here. I'm mad. You're mad.'

'How do you know I'm mad?' said Alice.

'You must be,' said the Cat, 'or you wouldn't have come here.'

Alice's Adventures in Wonderland.
Lewis Carroll.

Marketing is about which way to go, and how to get there. It has become an increasingly important part of business activity and yet it is extremely difficult to define exactly what it is. Part of the problem lies in the broad nature of the marketing function. The market now influences the whole process from raw materials to the finished product, affecting the development of the idea, the levels of production, the pricing of the product and the way it is presented and distributed to the final consumer. As such, it is a highly integrated function. In addition, marketing means different things to different people. For many, it is synonomous with advertising, partly because this is the most obvious public face of business, partly because it is the 'glamour' area of activity. For the sales staff, marketing is more likely to be viewed in terms of sales targets and selling techniques. To others it represents market research, finding out what the size of the market is and what competitors are doing, as well as the important part of discovering what consumers want and are prepared to buy. Marketing is all these things, and more. It is an all-embracing activity from the conception of the product to its final use, and an organisation can be made or broken by the way the marketing function is handled.

Marketing differs from other areas of business operation because of the uncertainty involved. Decisions are taken to introduce new products, mount advertising and promotion campaigns, develop and modify company and product images. For any chance of success, they require a major commitment of time and money well in advance of results. There is no guarantee of the outcome. There is no definite link between the inputs and the effects, and success is the result of the judgement of the marketing team based on past experience and the information obtained.

There is much more to a product than is immediately obvious. Biscuit manufacturers make biscuits, processing the raw materials to reach the desired end-product, namely, a biscuit. What they sell, however, is something more. If it was not, the manufacturer would find himself with a huge store of biscuits that remained at the factory. One of the areas of marketing involves the distribution of the product to the outlets where it is bought. Other areas involve image creation. All of them add value to the product.

When we purchase a packet of biscuits, we are buying something much more than a biscuit. Apart from the answer to questions such as 'Why did you buy that particular brand of biscuits?', consider the packaging itself. Clearly, one of the functions of packaging is to keep the product fresh, and intact. Secondly, it must be of a size that is suitable for the customer's needs, and easy for shops to handle. Thirdly, the product on the shelves is competing with other brands and types of biscuit for the customer's attention, so the package must be designed to be distinctive and easily noticeable, as well as reflecting the image the manufacturer wants the product to have. Bendicks 'Bittermints' are packaged to convey a sense of exclusiveness and quality; 'After Eight' Mints represent a lower priced attempt to do much the same thing for the mass market. If the package does not do its job well, then sales will be below their potential, reducing profits or, in the extreme case, causing the collapse of the product. Yet packaging is only one part of the whole marketing process.

1.2 The Change From Product-to Market-Orientation

In feudal times, society operated in small, self-sufficient units where the range of products available was largely determined by the resources at the disposal of the group. The needs of the group were basic – food, clothing and shelter, reflecting the base line of Maslow's hierarchy of needs (physiological, social, ego, self-fulfilment). These needs determined the priorities of production, but were so self-evident that marketing had no place in such societies.

With the advent of the Agricultural and Industrial Revolutions, the nature of production began to change. Specialisation and the division of labour meant that products could be manufactured in much greater numbers. Adam Smith cites an example of a firm making pins. Prior to the division of labour, output per man stood at 20 pins per day. Once the task had been split into two broad groups output per man rose to 4,000 pins per day. These changes were taking place against a background of rising population and longer life spans. Britain came to be the manufacturer for the world, importing raw materials and exporting manufactured goods. Britain's success at this stage marked the beginning of the need to take more notice of markets, because international competition began to grow from Germany and the United States. Just as improved transport and communications had enabled Britain to expand her markets, it also meant that she was, herself, a potential market for competitors' goods.

Mass production is generally recognised to have been pioneered by Henry Ford with his Model T. Yet the production of this car brought with it one of the earliest marketing strategies. In *My Life and Work*, Henry Ford says that he chose a price at which cars could be sold by the million, and then set about finding a way of producing them within this cost. Here, we have a clear example of market considerations determining production methods. It reflected a very different approach from the production-orientated firm, where the real problems lay in the means of producing goods. Market-orientation involves finding out what consumers want, and selling the product.

Mass production allows a reduction in the costs of each article produced through '**Economies of Scale**'. Although the **fixed overheads** of setting up a production line may be high, they are spread over a large number of units, so that provided there is sufficient demand for output each individual unit attracts only a small proportion of the total cost.

There are several types of economies of scale, including:

1. Managerial Economies.
In a large organisation it is possible to make use of specialists who are well qualified to advise in particular areas. An accountant, for example, is able to use his skills in the provision of detailed financial advice, both in the budgeting of future operations and in the control and review of past performance in the light of earlier budgets. Similarly, other functions within the firm can be organised by men or women trained in those specific areas. Such specialists are expensive, and usually only large organisations are able to finance and make full use of their services.

2. Marketing Economies.
In large-scale operations, bulk purchases of raw materials may be achieved at a lower unit rate, and economies may be obtained in distribution and promotion. A national market can be supported by a nationwide poster campaign, and this has a considerable reinforcing effect on potential customers.

3. Technical and Production Economies.
Costs do not necessarily rise proportionally with an increase in production capacity. A new blast furnace with twice the capacity of a small one will not cost twice as much to build since it will not require twice the materials. Equally, it will not cost twice as much to run, as less heat escapes into the fabric of the furnace in the larger one. It is more expensive to heat the same amount of water in two saucepans than in one large saucepan because there are two containers to heat.

4. Technological Economies.
Some technological developments require heavy investment in machinery. In the chemical industry much of the equipment is expensive, and only economic to use in large units. For example, recent developments in the fertiliser business enable profitable and efficient operation only if outputs are high. Large organisations are necessary for the benefits of new technology to be gained.

5. Financial Economies.
As firms increase in size, their needs for finance grow. However, the cost of finance may fall as loan size increases, and the ease with which loans are obtained will improve. Large organisations also have a wider variety of sources of finance, from the Stock Exchange and merchant banks, for example.

Production, as we know it now, altered radically after the Second World War. Huge organisations came into being, making vast numbers of products to fill the post-war consumer boom. However, after the initial rush when rationing was lifted, firms found themselves in a new situation. The seller's market eased and competition between firms became much stronger, both domestically and from overseas. Yet in order to reap the benefits of mass production it was necessary to sell large outputs, and consequently firms increasingly came to look more closely at their markets: at who was buying their products, at what changes their customers wanted, at the actions of their competitors, at the way they could best inform the public of their products and persuade them to buy. This was the real birth of marketing, and the change to market-orientation.

The standard of living rose as a result of this change. The benefits of specialisation, mass production and international trade have been greater productivity and greater wealth. That wealth has not always been evenly distributed, and governments have tried to do something to compensate for this through progressive direct taxation, social security benefits and welfare payments. However, regardless of its distribution, wealth could not have accrued at all had the markets for the increased output not opened up. Marketing became increasingly necessary to maintain and enlarge the market for a product.

A mass market is necessary for mass production to operate at a profit. Without it the cost advantages of economies of scale are lost, and products become more expensive. Higher prices reduce the size of the market and the number of people who can afford to buy products. The fall in demand leads to a reduction in output which has serious financial consequences for the firm, and represents a waste of the resources that are forced into idleness. Employment falls, and with it the material standard of living. At the same time, uncompetitive prices make foreign imports more attractive, so further reducing the demand for domestically manufactured goods. Since 1944, British governments have been committed to full employment and growth as two of their basic objectives. Marketing is an essential part of the process of achieving these ends.

1.3 The Importance and Need for Marketing

Many other factors contribute to the need for much greater interest in the market. As production lines become more sophisticated they cost far more to set up. This means that the cost of a failure is much greater. A firm which backs the wrong horse by making a product that people do not want, or is inferior to competitors' products, may not be able to survive. Certainly, profitability will be badly affected. Given that most organisations aim to make some profit or, at least, break even, time taken to sound out the market before undertaking major investment in plant and machinery is well employed. As in all expenditure, however, it is important to see that the cost of gathering the information on the market does not outweigh the benefits obtained from it.

It may take ten years or more for the idea of a new product to reach its finished state ready for consumers. Coupled with the cost of the production line and the rapid advance of technology, it is obviously essential to get the final product right. It is now too dangerous to leave the market to chance. Technical changes in the methods of manufacture and the materials that can be used, mean that firms must look ahead to discover new openings for existing products, and ideas which take advantage of new possibilities. The following case example illustrates the reaction of Kodak to the untapped market for cameras. By designing a product that matched consumers' needs it realised this potential market.

In the early 1950s Kodak was chiefly concerned with the professional photographic market, producing a limited range of cameras for the amateur, including its most famous, simple machine, the 'Brownie 127'. Aware of the tremendous potential market, the company undertook market research to discover more about the amateur photographer. It was surprised to find that half of the households it tested did not even possess a camera. The reasons for this lay in the use people wanted to make of photography. Most people wanted a camera to capture family scenes and holidays; they were not interested in the technical qualities of the final picture, nor did they want to involve themselves in complicated methods of taking pictures. Setting the aperture, the shutter speed and focus all affect the final picture but they also require a limited understanding from the photographer. Kodak found from its survey that it was this that prevented many families from buying a camera in the first place (and, of course, subsequently using other Kodak products – film, flashguns, etc.).

The major part of Kodak's product range was designed for twenty per cent of the market who were interested in the technical performance of their cameras. Even loading a film presented problems for potential customers so that the Brownie 127 failed to meet their needs. As a result of this, Kodak set about trying to design a system that would reduce the problems of loading a camera, and so open up a wide market. A new camera was developed that used a cartridge film which could be dropped into the camera without any threading problems. This camera, the Instamatic, was tested by employees and finally put on to the market. With nothing but a shutter to press it solved the 'snapshot' photographers' difficulties. Photography rapidly became a major hobby, providing huge sales for the manufacturer. Kodak then developed the Instamatic to incorporate a flash cube, removing the need to fit flash bulbs, and, more recently, a small camera that incorporates a hand grip, reducing camera shake and making it easier to hold. The cartridge idea has been extended to cine cameras with the growth of the 'home movie' market.

Firms can no longer rely on past products for future success. They must constantly adapt and improve. Past products may develop the image of the company: Rolls-Royce has a prestigious image from past cars, but this is not sufficient to enable it to sit back. Ideas of what is expected of a car change, and for Rolls to maintain its position in the market, it must anticipate change and be ready to capitalise on new developments. The market is moving increasingly quickly (see Fig. 1.1) and firms which are left behind face significant difficulties just to keep going.

Electric motor	65 years
TV	52 years
Vacuum tube	33 years
X-ray tube	18 years
Frozen foods	15 years
Nuclear reactors	10 years
Radar	5 years

Fig. 1.1: Time between invention and commercial development (*Source*: *Marketing*, by Baker)

As more products are made under conditions of intense competition and tight price margins, they tend to become very similar. For example, there are many different brands of washing powder or butter, all of which do much the same thing at nearly equivalent prices. It is important for firms to be as distinctive as possible in order to build up brand loyalty, and this has led to a greater emphasis on packaging and advertising. If a firm can make its name well known to consumers through advertising which links the product – say, Lager – with the brand – say, Carlsberg – then consumers are more likely to choose that brand since they have already heard of it. Firms work on this by introducing minor differences which distinguish one brand from its competitors – 'the blue whitener' of Daz or 'the mileage ingredient' of Shell. Once a purchase is made, a firm achieves its sale at the expense of every other manufacturer. This is particularly important in the field of consumer durables because a repeat purchase is unlikely to occur for some years. Hence there is increasing pressure on the market to persuade people to buy a particular brand. If a washing powder performs well and is up to the customer's expectations, then a measure of brand loyalty will be achieved, making it more likely that the replacement purchase will be made from the same firm.

As people's income rises, a wider range of possible purchases opens up. Figure 1.2 shows the change in ownership of consumer durables between 1965 and 1975 reflecting the increase in the standard of living. It means that firms have to persuade buyers that a new suit is preferable to a new refrigerator. Again, getting the product higher up the list of potential customers' preferences is a priority of advertising.

Thus there is a wide range of factors that have contributed to the need for a marketing function within the firm. The survival of the methods of production and the material benefits we have come to expect, depend on maintaining markets large enough to make use of improved technology at reasonable prices. There are many reasons for the development of the silicon chip, but the

	1965(%)	*1975*(%)
Percentage of households owning:		
Washing machine	56	71
Food mixer	8	40
Refrigerator	42	84
Toaster	16	28
Electric blanket	40	50
Vacuum cleaner	78	90
Central heating	16	49
Colour television	–	45
Freezer	–	21

Fig. 1.2: Ownership of consumer durables (*Source*: AGB, NOP)

calculator would never have been so inexpensive were it not for the rapid opening up of huge international markets. The costs of research and development as well as the investment in plant and machinery have been spread over a sufficiently large output to be barely evident in the total cost of an individual calculator.

1.4 Marketing: Summary and Definition

Marketing involves the examination of people's wants, and from this, the direction of production, the selling, packaging and distribution of the products once they are made. These wants in turn are dependent on the image of the product created in the customers' minds, hence the promotion, and the price. Marketing represents the link between producers and consumers (see Fig. 1.3). It is a highly integrated function, affecting all the other activities of an organisation. The products that should be made, and hence indirectly the types of skill, the size of the workforce and location of production, the priorities for finance and research, all depend in part, on the marketing function.

Broadly, goods are bought because they satisfy a need. Initially those needs are the basic physiological needs. After these have been satisfied consumers become more discriminating, and they buy products which satisfy emotional as well as physiological needs. Marketing is the process whereby the need is identified and then met. People buy perfume, not merely because they wish to 'smell nice' but because they feel that they are more attractive in some way. We may buy 'health' foods not primarily because we need food but because we want to live longer or suffer fewer diseases. Thus marketing comes to support far more than a simple product. It is a sophisticated process of satisfaction of a complex group of needs.

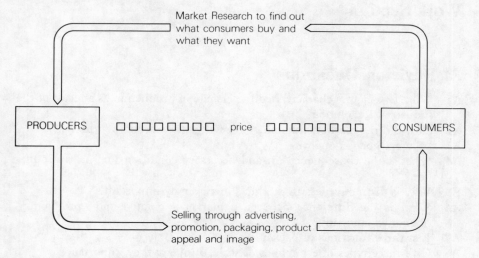

Fig. 1.3: The link between producers and consumers

Definition
'Marketing is an all-embracing function which assesses future market needs, co-ordinates the other functional areas of the firm (finance, production, research and development) to meet those needs, and promotes and distributes the goods or services at a price giving maximum satisfaction to the consumer, and profitability to the firm.'

Work Section

A. Revision Questions

A1 What two factors characterised the change in production as a result of the Industrial Revolution?

A2 How did the market situation change after the Second World War?

A3 Why are goods bought?

A4 What is the consequence of, and necessary condition for, mass production?

A5 Why is distinctiveness in products increasingly important?

A6 What is the difference between a market-orientated and production-orientated company?

A7 List three functions of packaging.

A8 Give three types of economies of scale. Why are they important?

A9 What is Market Research concerned with?

A10 Define Marketing.

C. Essay Questions

C1 Why has marketing become such an important part of business operations?

C2 What do you understand by the term 'market-orientation'? Why are firms organising themselves in this way?

C3 'Producers are specialists in production. Provided their products are of sufficient quality they will be successful. Marketing represents wasted resources.' Discuss.

Chapter 2

The Marketing Model

Objective: *To explain the various stages in the marketing model and their interrelationships.*

Synopsis: *The model brings together the various aspects of decision making in marketing. It provides a framework for creating a plan to execute the decisions taken on how to launch and develop a product as part of a product range. Company objectives give a broad direction to product policy. To achieve the full sales potential it is necessary to plan the marketing mix so that a coherent image is created, and the products are available at the right place and at the right time. The product range and marketing mix are modified to take account of changes in the market.*

Plan of the chapter:

2.1 Introduction

2.2 The Model in Detail

2.2.1 Objectives

2.2.2 Information and Analysis

2.2.3 Alternatives and Choice

2.2.4 Planning

2.2.5 Control and Review

2.1 Introduction

In Chapter 1 we looked at the general importance of the market to firms operating in competitive conditions. Even in a 'command' economy where a central planning agency decides what is to be produced, an analysis of consumer and industrial needs must be made to avoid surpluses and shortages of goods and services. This is even more important in a 'mixed' economy where consumers and competitive firms influence the range of goods that are produced. In general, for a firm to remain in business it must make something that people want and present it to the market in the best way possible. A formalised decision-making model can be developed and applied to the marketing decision.

The marketing decision model is set out in Fig. 2.1 and it serves as a framework for this book. In this chapter we look briefly at each stage of the

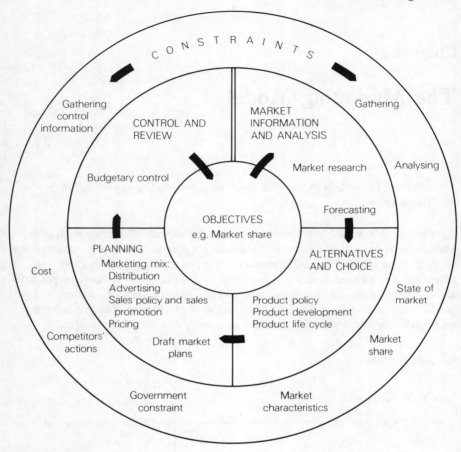

Fig. 2.1: The marketing model

decision and subsequent chapters go into greater detail. Organisations place differing importance on each part of the decision-making process depending on their size and importance in the market, but the broad approach can always be applied.

2.2 The Model in Detail

2.2.1 Objectives
Although marketing objectives are subservient to the overall aims of an organisation, their importance to the successful running of a business makes them an essential part of the strategic planning. Objectives are the ends the organisation is hoping to achieve. They provide direction for the operation and enable strategies, or the means to the ends, to be worked out. The type of product

made, the volume of output and the image of the product all influence the company's standing and the way it is viewed by others within industry and by the general public. The image of IBM is partly gained by the performance of its products and the quality and reliability they offer. Customers may be prepared to pay more for an IBM computer because the stature of the organisation gives them greater confidence than they would have with a less well known manufacturer of computer hardware. If quality is to be the hallmark of the product then from this strategic decision come a host of other tactical decisions such as price, service, product specification and so on. Similarly a decision to provide for a low-price, high-volume market, influences the overall

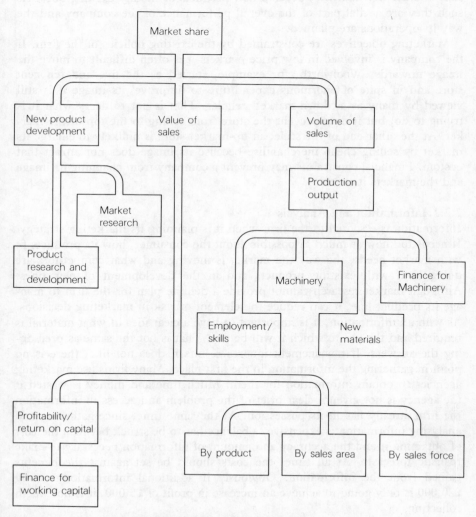

Fig. 2.2: A possible marketing objectives hierarchy

image of the company and puts different factors to the forefront of the marketing strategy.

Marketing objectives include targets for sales volume, market share, sales revenue, profitability and product development. They can be broken down by product, area and sales force. These numerate objectives then influence output, employment and finance requirements for capital and research expenditure and day-to-day operation (working capital). They affect the expected return on capital employed through pricing decisions which determine the volume of sales and the revenue obtained (see Fig. 2.2).

Marketing objectives follow from broader objectives surrounding the decision to enter new markets, develop new products or modify existing ones. As such they are a vital part of the overall performance of the company and the way its operations are planned.

Marketing objectives are constrained by the existing policies of the firm. If the company is involved in low price markets it is often difficult to move the image upwards. Woolworth, for example, started as the five and ten cent store and in spite of enormous expenditure to 'improve' its image it is still viewed by many as a 'down-market' retailer. That is not to decry what it is trying to do, but it does prevent the store from selling to the top of the market. At the other end of the scale, an up-market store is unlikely to enlarge its market by selling cheap merchandise because its image does not attract that custom. Financial constraints may prevent a company from changing its image and the markets it serves.

2.2.2 Information and Analysis

Information is essential to the firm when it is planning its marketing strategy. It needs to know as much as possible about the consumer, how its products fit with market needs, the way the market is moving and what competitors are doing both with existing products and in the development of new ones. Although market research cannot provide a definite plan for the firm to manage its product line, it can reduce the element of risk in marketing decisions. As with all information, it is important to have a clear idea of what material is required and the use to which it will be put. That is not the same as prejudging the answers. If management ignores results it does not like, there is no point in gathering the information in the first place. Many firms use marketing agencies to obtain information for them. Much time and money is wasted if the agency is not given a clear brief of the problem and access to information the firm already has in its possession. At the same time, since gathering and analysing information is expensive, a balance has to be struck between the cost of obtaining it and the accuracy and amount of information necessary to make realistic forecasts. At all times the costs should be set against the benefits gained from the information. Obviously if additional information costing £20,000 is only going to achieve an increase in profit of £5,000, it is not worth collecting.

There is usually a considerable amount of useful information that the firm already has. Past sales figures and profit provide a basis for analysing the performance of products in their markets. Internal information is less expensive than primary data obtained through interviews and questionnaires. The objectives of the firm and its past policy limit the market areas it can usefully consider. A small, specialist engineering firm can immediately eliminate mass produced spare parts from its range of product options unless it is to undergo a major reorganisation and shift of company policy. However, it should define its market so that it can classify the possible areas for product development. If the firm is currently making individual parts for vintage cars, it could widen its potential market by changing the market definition from 'owners of vintage cars' to 'people or organisations with specialist parts requirements'. From this, it may be able to use its skills to suppy parts for, say, the aviation industry. Often, market definition can throw up possible courses of action and new product areas for investigation. A company wishing to expand should constantly look for gaps in the market that it can fill.

Through retail and wholesale **audits** and indices the size of the total market and **market share** can be determined. The size of the market will depend on the type of product. Luxuries and specialist goods naturally sell in smaller quantities than necessities and mass-produced goods. It will also be influenced by the stage of the product in its life cycle. The **product life cycle** is a representation of sales through time reflecting the broad stages of development, growth, maturity and decline. Most products pass through such a cycle although sales levels and the time involved for each stage varies between different products. A mature product will face a reasonably static market before it declines with new technologies and styles rendering it obsolete. A successful new product will face a growing market. Given the productive capacity of the firm, **market potential** can be calculated. Market potential is the performance the firm should achieve if it uses its resources efficiently. In trying to achieve its market potential, the firm needs to know who its competitors are and how they are selling their products. It has to decide whether growth will come by taking sales from competitors or through expansion of the whole market. Different policies will be undertaken to achieve each of these possibilities. In deciding how it can expand its market the firm wants to know why people buy competitors' products and what is distinctive about them.

To make the most of the market, the firm needs as much information as possible on its actual and potential customers. Building a **'consumer profile'** which details the market by geographical location, income group, occupation, sex, age, purchasing habits, region and range of products purchased enables the firm to make informed decisions on how to distribute, promote and price its products.

There are many factors that influence sales such as price, tastes, income and availability of substitutes. One job of research is to monitor these so that the product range can be changed to suit new conditions. Testing of attitudes towards products and promotion schemes is constantly carried out to find the 'best' way of putting together a marketing package. Awareness levels of a product's existence and attributes determine whether a promotion campaign should be started, or packaging changed.

The purpose of the information obtained is to enable the firm to forecast future sales and plan its marketing strategy. Estimates of likely Government action which will alter the market, changes in taxation affecting income levels and prices, the level of activity in the economy which affects employment and consequently demand, movements in exchange rates affecting profitability from international trade and the extent of competition from imports, are all brought together to help build up a complete picture of the likely market position for the firm.

2.2.3 Alternatives and Choice

The findings of market research, and the internal information about the firm's ability to produce what the marketing department think consumers require are used to determine how best to alter the existing product range. Firms have to decide on the best use of limited resources when designing their product range and developments. They have to estimate the returns gained from, say, breaking into a new market or developing a new use for an existing product. At the same time demands are made to launch completely new products to replace those that are already being sold. In developing a product policy, a balance must be achieved between the short-term costs associated with new products and the long-term benefits from keeping ahead in the market and guaranteeing revenue into the future.

It is often difficult to decide whether to kill off a product which is still selling well, in order to launch a new one with good prospects. However, if the firm's resources will not cover both the cost of development of a new product and the cost of keeping an existing one on the market, the decision must be made. The product life cycle which charts the sales of a product against time can help in determining how it should be marketed. The product life cycle can be used to ensure that the product range is coherent and that the sale of all items within it are not about to decline at the same time. A company may have several groups of products within its total output and these groups are usually treated separately because they serve different markets. Black and Decker, for example, is heavily involved in industrial and do-it-yourself power tool markets. The characteristics of these markets are very different, one dealing in specialist requirements and the other in high-volume mass consumption. In addition, the nature of these markets has been changing with a growth in the size of the major manufacturers and a decline in small producers. The importance of the world market has increased and with it Black and Decker has moved away from tailoring its products to local markets towards design standards that are applicable throughout the world, so simplifying the product line. (A similar move has occurred in car manufacture where American safety and pollution standards, particularly, have led to changes in design world wide.)

At the same time, in response to the greater size of both power tool manufacturers and the markets it serves, Black and Decker has rationalised its product line so that those items which no longer provide sufficient profit have been abandoned or modified. In the light of technical change, particularly in microprocessors, motors and batteries, the product range is changing to make use of new developments. In this way the company makes a clear decision to drop products before competitors remove Black and Decker's market by introducing more up-to-date machinery themselves. Expertise in power tools has led to developments in other markets where similar technologies can be applied, such as in the medical field for sterilised tools to cut and drill bone.

The extent of the product research and development carried out by a company is usually determined by its size and its market share. If the firm is in a rapidly changing field, product research assumes greater importance. To maintain its market share the firm has to keep ahead of its competitors. If it is the market leader it is likely to innovate and set the pace for the rest of the firms in the industry. In line with research into products, market research is carried out to determine the way the product should be presented. At this stage ideas are tested on consumer panels to gain preliminary reactions to the product.

A market which is supplied by a few well-known brands is more difficult to enter than one with a wide diversity of producers. New firms, or ones entering the area for the first time, may encounter considerable difficulty in developing sufficient awareness for their brand to be able to sell it in volume. At the same time there is likely to be resistance in the distribution network because the new brand is an unknown quantity and it takes up valuable storage and display space. Enormous investment in marketing may be necessary to overcome the initial reluctance of both trade and consumers and the returns may not justify this cost. Promotion, selling and distribution methods for one market may be very different from another and a company with expertise in one product area may have very little to offer when it moves into a new type of market, as in the shift from industrial to consumer products.

The economic situation may also affect the options available to a company in developing its product range. At times of recession there is often greater reluctance to introduce new products because national spending power is down and the chances of a successful launch are consequently reduced. Similarly, other factors may affect a particular market. A change in fashion or priorities may cause a decline or expansion which can alter the decision to enter the market or increase the resources used to develop it.

2.2.4 Planning

With the information gathered on the market, and the historical data from inside the firm, a draft marketing plan is built up. It brings together the various aspects of the firm in relation to future product development and the direction it plots for the firm can be set against overall company objectives. Comparison of sales revenue and costs, the output required for sales and the capacity of the firm to meet this, the expenditure on marketing and an estimate of its return to the company all come together in the plan. This is followed by detailed planning of the presentation of the product to the market in the most successful way.

The strength of demand for a product can be significantly affected by the way it is handled in terms of its image, its availability, its performance and its price. The **marketing 'mix'** draws together these influences on demand. It is adjusted to provide a coherent policy towards the product. If different parts are in conflict, such as heavy advertising but poor distribution, then the full sales potential will not be reached. There is no single mix which will fit all products. It has to be tailored to the particular requirements of each product and market, and this will mean differing emphases on the constituent parts.

The main elements of the 'mix' include:

1. Distribution
Distribution covers the methods of bringing the product to the consumer and includes a wide range of possible channels, from direct links between manufacturer and consumer (common in industrial marketing and for some consumer goods sold directly through mail order), to a chain with middlemen such as **agents**, wholesalers and retailers. The firm has to decide the level of control it wants for its products up to the final point of sale, and the extent to which it can afford to finance stocking and distribution rather than leaving these functions to an experienced middleman.

2. Advertising
Designed to inform and persuade, advertising plays an important part in creating the image of a product. It adds value by enhancing the satisfaction obtained from using the product, and if sales volume is increased or maintained, economies of scale may enable the price to fall. Choices have to be made about the type of advertising and the media which will reach the largest relevant market creating a favourable impression. In addition, advertising is tailored for specific areas of the trade – wholesalers and retailers.

3. Sales Policy and Sales Promotion
The company has to decide how it proposes to sell its products into the trade and to the final consumer. This is closely linked with distribution policy but the size of the sales force, the incentives and the area to be covered will affect the volume sold. Trade fairs and special sales promotions are a vital part of getting a product accepted. The layout of stores, the packaging of the product and special offers influence the rate of sales. Branding is a way of creating distinctiveness which may give an edge over competitors and lead to a more constant market.

4. Pricing
The decision over the pricing of a product is critical because it determines the revenue for the firm. Price tells the consumer about the product as well as influencing the amount that is bought. Not all products are equally responsive

to price changes, but those with close substitutes must be priced at, or near, the competition if they are to achieve a reasonable market share.

The elements of the mix are affected by the type of product and the market for which it is intended. For example, fast-moving consumer goods tend to be promoted fully to ensure volume of sales is maintained and the choice of outlet and sales force is dependent on the buying habits of consumers. The size of the organisation and the resources available to it influence the extent to which it uses outside agencies to carry out its marketing function. A company with a national market may develop its own distribution network and use national advertising media to support sales. The market plan has to be suited to the state of the market. A growth market with new products being developed will be handled in a different way from one which is declining.

The mix is also heavily influenced by consumer and trade attitudes. The way consumers and the trade are motivated will determine the image for the product and the success with which it is taken up. Competitors' actions may alter the nature of the market and force a change in the priorities accorded to each part of the mix. If a major competitor increases his promotion substantially it may be necessary to spend more on advertising in order to maintain market share. Similarly a reduction in price may lead to a price-cutting war as different firms compete for the market.

The mix is constrained by Government action and legal controls. Thus certain forms of distribution are not allowed by law, advertising has both Government and voluntary controls which are designed to prevent exploitation. Unfair pricing by monopolies at the expense of the consumer is controlled by the Monopolies Commission, as are mergers of companies which may form organisations against the national interest. Prices and Incomes Policies reduce the flexibility of pricing strategies and the ability of companies to put up prices at will. A change in Government control can lead to a complete revamp of the marketing mix.

The mix allows flexibility in the market plan. For new products, **test markets** are sometimes undertaken to provide information on the consumers' reaction to the product and the way it is marketed. They can help finalise the design of the full launch by highlighting those parts of the mix that do not contribute to sales. The mix can be modified to take account of this information so that the 'mistakes' have been ironed out by the time the product is fully available.

2.2.5 Control and Review

Once a product has been launched, its progress is monitored against the sales objectives and its position within the product range. The marketing **budget** provides a yardstick for the cost involved in supporting the product in terms of sales force, advertising and administrative overheads. Movements in the market which influence the volume and value of sales are accounted for and where variances between budget and performance occur modifications are made in either objectives or the market plan. Measurement is complicated by the problems associated with gathering information. The analysis of figures to produce trends in sales and expectations should be used to provide an estimate of the long-term implications of the most recent results.

The function of control and review is to pick out variations from the planned outcome and then to analyse the reasons for them. There may be many causes for a difference between planned and actual performance. For example, a drop in sales may mean that competitors have produced a better or cheaper alternative, or it may be the result of a period of intensive consumer purchase which has temporarily left households with high stocks. Inflation and expectations of price increases might have caused this and the contrast in sales between the high purchasing month and the ensuing stock period will be all the more dramatic. Alternatively the drop in sales may be an indication that the market for the product is declining, in which case the firm has to decide how best to combat this.

The control function can only be as good as the original forecasts on which the budget was made, and the information-gathering system which produces a picture of actual performance. Budgets can be very detailed and they tend to reflect the structure of the marketing organisation. Thus a regional manager will have a breakdown of sales performance by sales personnel and sales territory, by advertising intensity, by special promotion and so on. Through these he will pick out any local discrepancies in planned and actual sales. In turn, the region will be analysed with others against targets set down by the divisional manager and so on, right through the organisation. The information and analysis of variances is then used as feedback to put right those factors, highlighted by the review, which are not working as they should be, or to modify objectives in the light of experience.

Work Section

A. Revision Questions

A1 List the stages of the marketing model.
A2 Distinguish between objectives and strategies.
A3 Give three examples of marketing objectives.
A4 Why is market information needed?
A5 What types of market information does the firm need and where can they be obtained?
A6 Why might a multi-national company standardise its product line?
A7 What problems do firms face when they enter a new market?
A8 What are the four main elements of the marketing mix?
A9 List four factors that influence the mix.
A10 What reasons could explain a decline in the sales of a product?

B. Exercises/Case Studies

B1 *The Launch of Persil Automatic*[1]
    Lever Brothers launched Persil Automatic in the UK in 1968. This case deals with the marketing decision surrounding that launch and is dependent on the information relevant to it. Since 1968 many factors have changed but they do not concern the decision taken at that time.

    Lever Brothers is part of Unilever, a multi-national company, manufacturing a wide range of mass-consumer products, in the cleanliness and hygiene market. Soaps and detergents for fabrics, dishwashing, household cleaning and personal washing make up the bulk of its range. The objective of the company, in common with many other commercial enterprises, is to make products that satisfy consumer needs at prices which will yield reasonable profit and growth in both the short and long term.
    In 1970 the UK washing powder market was the largest that Lever Brothers operated in with a total market volume of ⅓ m. tons per annum (exclusive of industrial and laundering trade requirements). At that time there were around 18 m. households each buying about 26 packets of

---

[1] This case has been adapted from the Unilever booklet of that name by Paul Garwood (No. 2 of the Introduction to Business Studies), by kind permission of the author and Unilever.

washing powder each year, creating a total market of £85 m. at 1970 prices.

The market, because of its size, is highly competitive and this has implications for pricing and product characteristics. The two major manufacturers for the UK were Lever Brothers and the American company Procter and Gamble Ltd. In addition, Colgate Palmolive, an American multinational with a UK organisation, and Henkel, an expanding German company, both had the potential to develop branded products for Britain and were watching for the right conditions for entry into the market. There had also been significant growth in 'own brands' sold by multiples and supermarket chains.

Although the annual tonnage of washing power had remained fairly constant over the previous fifteen years, this masked considerable growth in the fabric washing market because of the development of specialist products for dishwashing and household cleaners. Washing-up liquid, for example, had largely replaced powders and was selling over 100,000 tons per year. Powders were almost exclusively used for washing fabrics.

Detergent prices had not risen as fast as inflation because of the intense competition within the market and the need to maintain a high volume of sales to cover overheads, and the agreement to restrict price increases following an investigation by the Monopolies Commission and the Prices and Incomes Board in 1967.

Lever Brothers has to balance costs and revenue to make a profit. However, because it is part of a multi-national company much of the research and development carried out in the UK goes towards products sold in markets throughout the world. The same product with modifications for local conditions and preferences contributes to the overall return on capital of the company. An attempt to make too much profit by pricing high is likely to lead to a declining market share and the margins are restricted as a result of competitive pressure. Furthermore, tight margins make the market less attractive to new competitors. High fixed overheads mean that a fall in sales can easily change a profit into a loss, and excessive profits will encourage competitors to break into the market, so reducing the advantages of economies of scale. In addition to production overheads, research and marketing costs can only be borne by high volume sales. Thus pricing decisions have to be taken with the long-term picture in mind. The development of products to meet new market needs is also vital if the company is to remain ahead of competition.

Market research plays an important part in keeping the company at the forefront of sales. Monitoring the use of its products and attitudes towards them enables Lever Brothers to modify and develop its range as the market changes. It is difficult to determine exactly what consumers are looking for in a washing powder. The ability to clean clothes is obviously the general objective, with whiteness allied to cleanness. This is only part of the picture since care of clothes and coloured fabrics, the ability to remove stains easily and the 'softness' of the washed garment are also important. Features such as perfume, pack design and product appearance influence the purchasing decision and the consumer's satisfaction with the product, although they are less obvious than the performance of the powder. As the market has grown, more specialised detergents have been developed to deal with specific requirements. Biological washing powder, or the long standing brand of soap flakes 'Lux', are examples. A general powder for a wide range of fabrics has to compromise between the various requirements, and the method of its use affects its performance. The type of washing machine used, the amount of powder, the extent to which clothes are sorted before they are washed and the length of the wash all alter the success with which clothes are cleaned. Even now, with detailed washing instructions in most garments there is relatively little sorting into categories.

Washing machines have come to play an important part in the cleaning of clothes. The type of machine determines the type of powder that should be used. Front-loading automatics require a low lather product because unlike the top loaders and non-automatic machines there is only a limited quantity of water for the lather to rest on and the washing action is vigorous. If a high lather powder is used the water in the machine can overflow and in extreme cases the machine will stop altogether. By using less powder the ability to clean is reduced, hence it was vital for Lever Brothers to analyse ownership of machines in the market.

In 1969, 60 per cent of the UK households owned washing machines and this was growing at about 2 per cent p.a. Of these less than 10 per cent were automatics, both top and front loading. In America ownership was nearer 95 per cent, all of which were automatic. Research findings gave the information below:

Ownership of front loading automatic machines

	Per cent of households	
	1962 (%)	*1969 (%)*
UK	1	5
Holland	5	25
France	15	35
Italy	10	40
W. Germany	18	52

The growth in front-loading machines was largely the result of pressure from Italian manufacturers. Cheaper to manufacture than top loaders, they had rapidly replaced the old 'twin-tub' machines. It was likely that sales in the UK would rise and the possibility of membership of the EEC (Britain actually joined in 1973) enhanced this. In the mid 1960s, however, Britain's market for low lather powders was small and the company had to decide whether to manufacture a product specifically for this minority group. There was one low lather brand but it was relatively unknown and not widely available.

If Lever Brothers were to take advantage of the potential market and keep its products up to new consumer needs it had to launch a low lather powder. Persil was already a well established brand of soap powder and had a close association with top-loading machines where it performed well. Since the 1950s it had been recommended by washing machine manufacturers, and the decision was taken to produce a product specially formulated for front-loading automatics. In Europe other Unilever companies had already been working on this problem, and Lever had the advantage of their experience in product design and marketing strategy. The choice lay between starting a new brand and using a variant of the existing brand, Persil.

A new brand would give maximum flexibility in designing all aspects of the product to meet the consumer need. It would be uncluttered by associations with Persil and would avoid confusion between automatic and non-automatic brand. However, starting a new brand would require enormous marketing resources to gain sufficient awareness and to sell it into the distribution trade. Brand image is the consumers' view of the whole product, its performance and how best to use it. The market had several well established products with clear brand images and a new brand would have to compete against these.

The alternative was to use a variant of an existing brand which would have the advantage of a well established image and lead to economies of scale in marketing. In addition there would be an improvement in the parent brand's image which would be enhanced by the new product. Promotion of one would increase awareness of both brands. But there was always the danger of confusion in the consumers' mind as to which product would be the most suitable for their needs. At worst, use of the wrong product would produce poor results which might lead to rejection of Persil altogether. Much of the market might come from existing Persil users so that total market share would not rise.

Against this background Lever decided to introduce a new brand, 'Skip', in a test market in mid-1966. In setting up the brand and test market it was able to use its existing knowledge of the European market. As ownership of front-loading automatics grew so the investment in the brand would increase. Research was carried out to discover the consumer profile of potential users of the brand and although certain publications which had a large proportion of the target market were isolated, there did not seem to be much coherence in their shopping habits. This meant that distribution would be at a low level initially and would grow with brand acceptance. The Yorkshire TV area with 10 per cent of the UK population was chosen as the test market.

The results of this test were disappointing, with lower brand awareness and distribution than had been expected. In the light of this, television advertising was started and incentives introduced for the distributor to handle the product. Sales and awareness improved but the return was still too low to justify the cost, so the brand was dropped. In its place the company gave higher priority to the development of a variant of an existing brand. As with 'Skip', Persil Automatic was started in a test market. The Southern Television area was chosen for its relatively high ownership of front-loading automatics and because Persil was not such a strong brand there. This would minimise the chance of confusion. The price of Persil Automatic was higher than the standard Persil partly because the cost of the materials was higher and partly because the size of the market meant that major economies of scale could not be achieved. The television advertising stressed the differences between Persil and Persil Automatic and was essentially educational in its approach, emphasising its suitability for the new type of washing machines. Trade acceptance of the product was higher because of the link with Persil and a wide distribution was achieved.

In this environment, sales grew rapidly and research showed there was little confusion between the two brands. As a result of this the decision was taken to launch the brand nationally and by 1970 it had become the only major brand recommended for front-loading machines. However, as the market grew with increased ownership of automatic washing machines it was inevitable that competitors would develop their own automatic powders. At the same time a careful reallocation of resources between Persil and Persil Automatic would have to be carried out as their relative importance changed.

Question

Using the stages of the marketing model (Fig. 2.1), explain carefully how they apply to the launch of Persil Automatic.

C. Essay Questions

C1 A company is considering manufacturing a new hi-fi product. How would you advise it to organise the marketing function?

C2 'Marketing is about doing. All theoretical approaches are irrelevant'. Discuss.

C3 How does the marketing model clarify the way decisions are taken?

Chapter 3

The Demand For Goods

Objective: *To examine the theoretical approach to demand; to consider the determinants of demand and limitations of the theoretical approach; to introduce the concept of elasticity.*

Synopsis: *As part of the overall marketing policy we need to consider what factors affect people's purchasing decisions. The firm is interested in effective demand and how it is influenced by changes in the determinants of demand.*

Plan of the chapter:

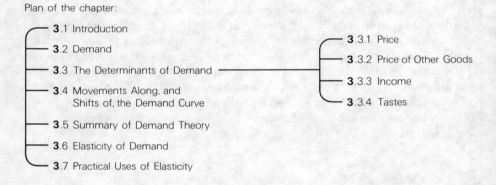

3.1 Introduction

When a firm is planning a marketing policy, first and foremost it needs to discover something about the market it is to operate in. This involves knowledge of actual and potential consumers and what they want from a product, and also what makes people choose one product rather than another. Many successful firms have started by finding a gap in the market, either because existing manufacturers have not attempted to sell to a particular group in society or because they have seen the possibilities of exploiting a new idea. Gathering information on the market is known as Market Research. In this chapter we shall look at the factors affecting the demand for a product from a theoretical standpoint.

Economists have developed a sizeable body of demand theory. One of the problems is that in practical situations people do not always react in the way theory suggests. Nevertheless, an appreciation of the basic determinants of demand is essential before we modify the theory to suit the particular requirements of a firm. Demand theory is based largely on the concept of '**economic man**'. Fundamental to this is the view that man is rational and acts to achieve maximum economic gain, so in order to reach a decision we must have access to all the information relevant to that decision. If we consider price as a factor that affects demand, the choice between a range of similar products will be made in terms of all the possible prices and the benefits each product confers. Clearly, a theory based on such premises will not necessarily work in practice.

3.2 Demand

In Chapter 1 we talked of physiological needs – food, clothing and shelter – needs for those things which enable us to live. However, there are many ways in which we can satisfy these needs. When someone is hungry he has a need for food; he can satisfy his hunger by eating fish or meat or eggs and so on. The fact that there are different ways of answering a need means that a choice has to be made, and the choice will be influenced by many things: for example, tastes, what he has eaten most recently, the time he has to prepare food and many other individual reasons. He may decide that he wants a treat, or his budget may be running low so that he must choose cheaper foods. A multitude of economic, social and physiological factors come together to determine the final choice. Once the decision is made there is a specific want as opposed to need.

We have many wants, but not all of them can be met. All sorts of things we want may be too expensive for us or too low on our priorities. I may want a fast car but because I have to pay the rent or a mortgage repayment or the heating bill, I cannot afford to buy the car. The world can only produce a limited amount of goods or services and wants will always outstrip the ability to produce so we are forced to choose between our wants.

A want backed by the ability to pay is known as **effective demand**[1] and it is this demand that we shall be examining. Generally, the firm wishes to influence our priorities so that what it produces is near the top of the list. There are occasional situations where this does not apply. The Government is exhorting

---

[1]Technically, demand falls into three categories:
1. Effective demand – demand backed by the ability to pay.
2. Potential demand – where there is the ability to pay but demand has not been aroused.
3. Latent demand – demand for goods not backed by the ability to pay.

us to save energy and could apply pressure through the British National Oil
Corporation which, while wanting us to use its product is also trying to persuade us to use it efficiently. However, for the most part, firms use advertising
as a means of influencing our priorities. 'Guinness is good for you' tells us that
we will be doing ourselves a favour if we drink Guinness, thus competing with
Coca Cola which is 'the real thing', and so designed to appeal to our practical,
rational selves. In turn, these products are competing with all other goods such
as after-shave – 'makes a man of you' – working on our vanity.

A firm is interested in the total demand for its product. That total demand is
made up of all the individual demands. The fact that your demand for chocolate bars is largely independent of their price, while mine varies sharply with
the price is only of interest to us as individuals. It does not mean that we
cannot produce a general relationship between demand for a product and its
price. It is reasonable to say that demand for chocolate bars varies with price if
the overall market shows such a relationship. Firms are concerned with the
whole market and not an individual response to price. We can make general-
ised statements without requiring everyone to match them exactly.

3.3 The Determinants of Demand

To find out the factors that affect the demand for a product requires observa-
tion, and analysis of the findings. Consider the demand for Mars bars. For
most people, demand will vary according to the price of each bar. The lower
the price, the more bars will be bought. Of course, there is a limit to how far
this can go – a surfeit of chocolate bars has undesirable consequences. In addition to price there are many other factors that influence demand. Income is a
significant constraint. The demand for Mars bars is affected by the price of
other chocolate bars so that Mars has to consider the prices of competitors'
products when deciding its own price. Taste, too, has a considerable impact on
demand – we may simply not like a particular chocolate bar. It is obviously
difficult to decide which variable is most important. All are operating to some
degree at the same time, and some play a bigger part in determining demand
for one product rather than another. When we are looking at different
detergents the relative prices play an important part in the choice, but when
we consider perfume, or a record player, taste may be more significant. To
overcome this problem of many factors affecting demand at once, the situation
is simplified. As each determinant of demand is looked at, we assume all other
factors remain constant. Thus we might consider the effect of price on demand
while holding income, advertising and competitors' actions constant. While
this may appear unrealistic, it is common scientific practice to examine one
area under laboratory conditions, so giving us a clearer idea of what is going
on, and from this to generalise. Once we understand the part played by each
determinant, we are in a better position to see how they interact.

The main determinants of demand are:
1. Price
2. Price of other goods
3. Income
4. Taste

Factors affecting the ability to purchase

Affects willingness to purchase.

Let us now look at the factors in more detail.

3.3.1 Price

We buy goods because they fulfil a particular requirement; that is, they satisfy a need. We also have a strongly developed sense of value, often subjective, but clear to ourselves. Thus we choose one product which is less expensive than another because it represents 'good value'; we are pleased when we have managed to get a 'bargain'; at certain times of the year cauliflowers are a 'good buy' because they are cheaper than usual. In each case we judge our success in purchasing by comparing what we have bought with price. We have already noted that the number of chocolate bars we might buy in a week is partly dependent on price. Why is this so? Why would we not buy as many bars at a high price as we would at a lower one? The reasons lie in the satisfaction we get from consuming each bar. Usually we get the most satisfaction from the first bar we eat; the second, although good, is not so interesting as the first, so presumably we would not wish to pay as much for the second. In addition, having had one bar, we are more likely to consider buying something else with our money – thus there is competition between different types of goods for our limited resources. In order to make us buy two bars (i.e. increase effective demand) the firm has to reduce the price, so that the satisfaction per penny remains the same.

Of course, the individual decision to buy is much more complex than this, and much of the thinking is subconscious so that we do not add up the 'units of satisfaction' and compare with price in an obvious way. Nevertheless, there are occasions when we do think consciously about purchasing a large packet of

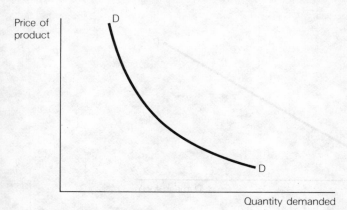

Fig. 3.1: A demand curve

washing powder rather than a smaller one by comparing the weights and prices of the two packets.

We can show the relationship between the demand for a product and its price graphically (other things remaining the same).

The shape and gradient of the 'demand curve' depends on the nature of the product, whether it is a luxury or a necessity as well as what alternatives are available. This is examined more fully in section **3.6**.

3.3.2 Price of Other Goods

In addition to its own price, the demand for a product is also affected by the price levels of other goods. The demand for a particular make of cassette will depend partly on the price of other cassettes on the market (as well as their quality). This is because most cassettes offer similar characteristics but at different prices, and as such they are substitutes. The existence of close substitutes makes a manufacturer very susceptible to the actions of his competitors because demand easily switches from one product to another. If the price of one washing powder rises, while others remain the same, demand will tend to move away from the more expensive brand to its cheaper competitors unless there are definite reasons for it not doing so. Hence firms try hard to prevent **'brand substitution'** by giving their own product some special characteristic. 'Ariel washes better because it washes biologically'; 'Daz the blue whitener', suggest specific attributes, so building up a brand loyalty which gives the manufacturer more independence to follow his own policies. Because consumers do switch between brands, it is a firm's prime marketing consideration to make sure its brand is always available on the shelves in a store. Thus when *The Times* was not being produced because of an industrial dispute, the management had to consider the consequences of readers changing to another newspaper and not returning to *The Times* when it started production again. Similarly, any change in the brand, either in its content, packaging, size or price, has to be taken against the likely reaction of its customers, and their

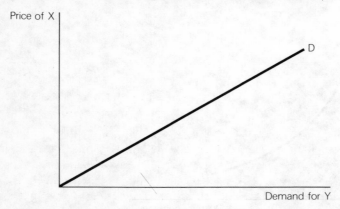

Fig. 3.2: Demand for a product dependent on the price of substitute.

subsequent purchasing decisions. The closer the substitute, the more important these factors are. The relationship between two substitutes X and Y is shown in Fig. 3.2.

In addition to brand substitution, there is also substitution between products. At its simplest level, the two products are similar. We might switch from butter to margarine, or from fresh to frozen vegetables. While these changes have an enormous impact on a manufacturer of foodstuffs, the competitive market is reasonably clear. However, **product substitution** can be extended far more widely; we might substitute the purchase of a new suit for a record player, or a second-hand car for a holiday. Here we are considering products which are not similar at all. Certainly they are not substitutes in the usual meaning of the word, but they do compete for the household's limited purchasing power. After the oil price increase in 1973 manufacturers of electrical goods found that demand for their products fell as people used their income to buy more expensive petrol, leaving less available for the purchase of washing machines and other electrical goods. This reflects the fact that the demand for petrol as a whole does not vary significantly with price, although the demand for a particular brand may be very price dependent (see Fig. 3.3). It also underlines the need for firms to promote their products, not just to prevent sales from being captured by direct competitors but also to keep the actual product high in the list of priorities.

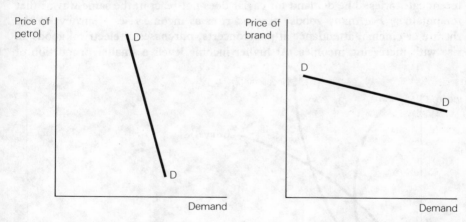

Fig. 3.3 (i): Demand for petrol   Fig. 3.3 (ii): Demand for a particular brand of petrol

There is another category of goods which faces 'joint demand'. Petrol and cars are two products whose demand is closely connected. They are known as complements because a change in the price of one directly affects the demand for the other. A complement is a product which involves the use of other products. When the price of petrol rose there was an increase in the demand for smaller cars (see Fig. 3.4) and a reduction in demand for large cars.

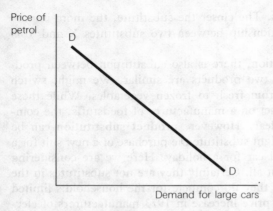

Fig. 3.4: Demand curve for a complementary product

3.3.3 Income

Income is a very important factor in the determination of the demand for a product. As with price, the nature of the goods will affect the way demand for it depends on income. The demand for salt does not rise dramatically with increases in income, nor does it fall when incomes fall. This is true up to a point with many necessities, although foods, for example, have distinctly different categories. The demand for caviar does not react in the same way as that for potatoes. For many goods, demand rises as income rises. Journeys to the theatre or cinema, attendance at pop concerts, purchases of electrical goods all rise with increasing incomes. At higher income levels a smaller proportion of

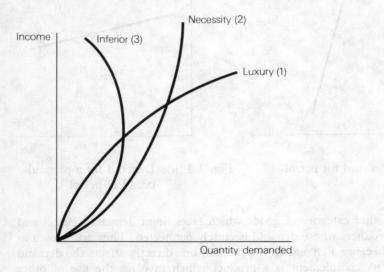

Fig. 3.5: Income-demand curves

our total income is used on the purchase of necessities, and consequently purchases of non-essentials rise. Since the early 1950s incomes in the West have
grown considerably, and a much wider range of goods has been purchased.
Firms have been aware of this change and benefited from it. Many have taken
particular care to ensure that they have received some of the increasing expenditure by making goods which are attractive to consumers and preferable to
competitors' products. It has also led to the growth of methods of persuading
people to buy one product and brand rather than another.

In Fig. 3.5 there are three income/demand graphs. The demand for luxuries
(1) varies with income. At low levels of income little is used on luxuries since
essentials (2) such as food and clothing, claim most of the household's earn-
ings. As income rises the demand for luxuries rises sharply but there is no
significant change in the demand for necessities. We do not spend more on
milk when income rises, once we have sufficient to keep body and soul
together.

Inferior goods (3) are products which face a decline in demand after a certain level has been reached. Potatoes might be such a product. When income
levels are very low potatoes form an important part of the household's diet.
However, when income rises they may be replaced by meat as a food source.
Such a shift shows potatoes to have the characteristics of an 'inferior good'.
'Inferior' used in this sense in no way implies that one product is less 'good'
than any other. It is a label attached to a particular demand pattern shown by
that product.

3.3.4 Tastes

Tastes and fashions play a significant role in determining the level of demand
for a product. Taste is a personal thing – it may be that we don't like cabbage,
and for that reason we will not buy it; or we may not like travelling by bus.
Equally, many goods become fashionable or unfashionable. Whether we like it
or not, most of us are affected by fashions or crazes, and we buy things that
perhaps in a year will be seldom used. Hoola-hoops became a major craze in
the late 1950s and there was a sudden demand for them; more recently there
was a craze for skateboarding. Some crazes remain for longer periods. Clothing
is subject to trends: hemlines on skirts go up and down, jackets have wide or
narrow lapels, trousers are flared or narrow. Jeans, on the other hand, have
stayed with us for a long time although styles have changed. Trying to influence fashions through promotion and advertising is part of daily experience,
and very important to the company which is rising on the crest of a fashion
wave, or trying to create a market for a new idea.

Understanding the way people follow fashions requires a knowledge of
psychology. Firms need to discover why people's tastes change. For our purposes we are principally concerned with the fact that they do change and the
influence that a change is going to have on the demand for a product.

3.4 Movements Along, and Shifts of, the Demand Curve

Let us return to the basic demand curve, which shows the relationship between price and demand. A demand curve only holds true when all factors other than price remain constant. Changes in price create movements *along* the curve. In Fig. 3.6 where price falls from p_1 to p_2 the quantity demanded by consumers rises from q_1 to q_2. The movement is along the curve from A to B. Any change in factors other than price will lead to a *shift* of the curve. Thus if incomes rise the demand for some goods will rise at all price levels. This is shown by an outward shift of the curve from DD to D'D'.

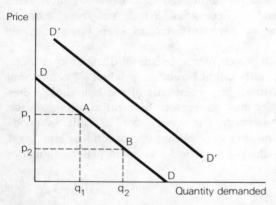

Fig. 3.6: Shifts of, and movements along, the demand curve

3.5 Summary of Demand Theory

The demand theory we have developed is the result of general observations. Individuals make purchasing decisions for many reasons and exceptions to the general trends can always be found. A miser whose income rises may not spend any more than the minimum to cover basic essentials. Some people will go without many so-called necessities in order to indulge in the occasional luxury. However, research has shown that people, in general, do conform to the sort of behaviour suggested in the chapter. In spite of the fact that the analysis is static (i.e. only one variable is allowed to change at a time) the general information is of use to firms in a changing market situation because it provides a greater understanding of the way in which different forces affect demand, and it may point to areas where problems arise.

We saw that demand was dependent on price, income, the price of all other goods (some more than others) and on tastes. Inevitably the nature of the product also affects the kind of demand it faces. But there are also many other factors which influence demand; for example: levels of taxation or subsidy which affect prices, Government intervention directly through rationing, advertising and pressure selling, credit facilities through hire purchase sales, credit cards and trade credit which affect the income/demand relationship.

There are many sophisticated theories of demand which attempt to include some of these other factors. The relative income hypothesis, for example, looks at how the purchases of a particular group affect the individual household behaviour, a sort of 'keeping up with the Joneses' concept. This is not the place to discuss them but they can be found in any advanced economics text book.

One of the problems that bedevils practical application of demand curves is the complexity of the information required to produce exact relationships for particular products. An enormous amount of information is required which is difficult and costly to obtain with sufficient accuracy. Once a demand curve is produced there is no guarantee that other factors will not change and invalidate the relationship. In the next section we examine by how much demand for a product will change when factors affecting it change.

3.6 Elasticity of Demand

We have already seen that the shape of the demand curve varies between different products. The demand for salt does not change significantly with price or income, whereas the demand for one brand of washing powder is greatly affected by its price relative to close substitutes. The measure of how responsive demand is to price is known as the price elasticity of demand. Demand is more likely to be responsive (elastic) to price when the product represents either a major purchase which can be delayed, or one that has close substitutes. A rise in the price of a television set might postpone the decision to buy a new one or alter the choice of manufacturer. Choosing between different makes of television is usually a carefully thought out process. It is less likely to be the case for a packet of cereal. If we are considering other determinants of demand we will consider different elasticities. Thus products whose demand is more responsive to income are said to have a greater income **elasticity** of demand.

Elasticity is a measure of the responsiveness of one variable to a change in another variable. It can be used qualitatively or quantitatively. Businessmen are interested to discover by how much the demand for a product will change when the factors that affect demand alter. For example, given the growth in real income in Britain since the war, many firms will want to know by how much they can expect purchases of their products to increase. Similarly, if a firm is considering changing the price of one of its products it will want to have some estimate of how sales will be affected. A change in the price of other goods, complements or substitutes, will affect the demand for a product to a greater or lesser extent. If firms can obtain sufficient information they can compare the percentage changes in demand with percentage changes in price.

Thus:

$$\text{Price elasticity of demand} = \frac{\%\ \text{change in quantity demanded}}{\%\ \text{change in price}}$$

$$\text{or}\quad \text{Income elasticity of demand} = \frac{\%\ \text{change in quantity demanded}}{\%\ \text{change in income}}$$

$$\text{or}\quad \text{Cross elasticity of demand} = \frac{\%\ \text{change in quantity of A demanded}}{\%\ \text{change in price of B}}$$

Because this involves a comparison of percentages, elasticity has no units.

Example: A small firm making wooden toys wishes to increase its sales, by reducing the price from £1.50 per article to £1.20. Having done this, the firm found that sales rose from 400 toys to 600. What is the price elasticity of demand?

$$\textit{Price elasticity of demand} = \frac{\textit{\% change in toys demand}}{\textit{\% change in price}}$$

$$\begin{aligned}\textit{\% change in toys demanded} \\ \textit{(i.e. sales)}\end{aligned} = \frac{600-400}{400} \times 100\ = 50\%$$

$$\textit{\% change in price} = \frac{£0.30}{£1.50} \times 100\ = 20\%^1$$

$$\textit{Thus price elasticity of demand} = \frac{50\%}{20\%} = 2.5$$

This tells the firm that demand changes by 2.5 times as much as price over this price range. In other words, demand is responsive to price. When elasticity is greater than one we say that the demand for the product is elastic; when elasticity is less than one the demand is inelastic. In the example of the toy manufacturer we saw that the demand for the product was elastic. In such a situation lowering the price will lead to an increase in total sales revenue.
400 toys @ £1.50 were sold: Total revenue = £600
600 toys @ £1.20 were sold: Total revenue = £720

In this case, if the elasticity had been less than one, total revenue would have fallen as price was reduced. This is because the demand would not have increased proportionately by as much as the price fell. It is worth noticing that elasticity usually varies over the whole range of the demand curve. This can be seen in terms of total revenue.

---

[1] Since the change in price is a fall the percentage change should be −20 per cent, giving a price elasticity of demand of −2.5. However, since nearly all products face some diminution in demand when prices rise, it has become the practice to drop the minus when referring to price elasticity of demand.

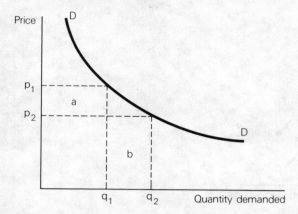

Fig. 3.7 (i): Change in total revenue when price falls

In Fig. 3.7 (i) the price has fallen from p_1 to p_2 and total revenue has been reduced by the area (a) but the demand has risen from q_1 to q_2, so increasing revenue by the area (b). Since the area of (b) is larger than (a), overall revenue has risen. Over this price range the demand is elastic. This is confirmed by comparing the change in price (from the diagram about 15%) with the change in quantity demanded (about 40%). In Fig. 3.7 (ii) on the same demand curve we see that total revenue has fallen, showing that over this lower price range demand is inelastic. Thus the elasticity of a demand curve varies over its length. Figure 3.7 (iii) shows the range from elasticity at high prices to inelasticity at low prices. A small drop in price at the left-hand end of the curve leads to a significant increase in total revenue. A similar reduction in price at the right-hand end of the curve leads to a fall in revenue.

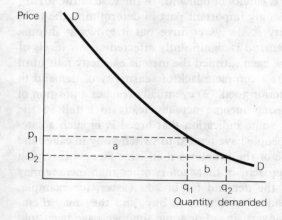

Fig. 3.7 (ii): Change in total revenue when price falls

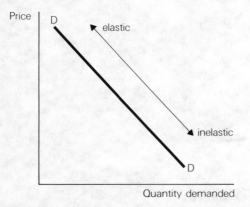

Fig. 3.7 (iii): Changing elasticity of a demand curve

It is important not to confuse revenue with profit. Although total revenue may rise (as in Fig. 3.7(i)) we are told nothing about costs. If we were only just covering costs at p₁ and costs rise proportionally with output, then lowering the price, although increasing sales, will do so by selling at below cost. Elasticity concerns total revenue only.

Products which have close substitutes face more elastic demand curves than those with no near alternative. This means that manufacturers of instant coffee, for example, find their sales are very susceptible to price changes both of their own and of competitors' products. In this case we can develop the idea of cross-elasticity which reflects the responsiveness of demand for one product to change in the price of its substitute.

In Fig. 3.5 we saw how demand for a product is dependent on income. The three curves reflected three different categories of goods, and we can now explain them in terms of income elasticity of demand. In the case of the luxury good (1) income plays an increasingly important part in determining the level of demand. The income elasticity is always positive but it grows as income rises. For most necessities (2) demand is significantly affected at low levels of income but once basic needs have been satisfied the income elasticity falls until it reaches near zero. This reflects a complete lack of sensitivity of demand to income at higher levels. The 'inferior good' (3) eventually reaches a position of negative elasticity where increasing income actually leads to a fall in the demand for a product. There is some indication that bread is in such a category since with higher incomes people have tended to switch away to cakes and biscuits. This also illustrates one of the problems that firms face when trying to make use of the elasticity approach, in that factors other than income may have been at work in changing the demand for bread. Tastes, for example, may have changed, making bread a less attractive buy, and they may themselves have been influenced by advertising. For some time we have been told that 'Mr Kipling bakes exceedingly good cakes'.

3.7 Practical Uses of Elasticity

In trying to make use of the concept of elasticity in business, firms are faced with significant problems. Apart from the difficulty and expense of obtaining sufficient information to derive elasticity values, in the real world many variables are changing simultaneously. Consequently, it becomes necessary to calculate several different elasticities and the effects of each on the other. Suppose a firm was finding it very difficult to sell its product. The marketing director decided to lower its price and also to increase advertising expenditure so that he could publicise the greater value of the product. At the same time his major competitor was finding that the costs of production were increasing and put up prices. After a while the marketing director of the first firm was able to announce increased sales of his product, but he was unable to determine the extent of the effect of each factor. To do so he would have needed to know, amongst other things, the following:

- By how much demand increased as a result of the reduction in price (price elasticity of demand).
- By how much demand increased as a result of increased advertising expenditure (advertising elasticity of demand).
- By how much demand increased because both price fell and advertising increased at the same time.
- By how much demand increased because of the increase in his competitor's price (cross elasticity of demand).

Thus it becomes extremely difficult to used exact, quantitative elasticity in business situations. However, this does not mean that the concept has no value for business. Firms need to know in what broad range their products fall. Since the Second World War incomes have risen and this has considerably affected sales. A firm will want to know how such changes will alter different products: whether it is manufacturing an inferior good and into what possible areas it should diversify. During this period costs of production have risen and are in part passed on through higher prices. The extent to which these increases can be reflected in the final price depends on the responsiveness of the demand for a product to its price, and the actions of competitors faced with similar difficulties. If the cross elasticity is high then it will benefit the company, in terms of the share of the total market, to keep prices down. The concept of elasticity is valuable because it underlines the importance of examining the market when setting prices or determining marketing expenditure.

Work Section

A. Revision Questions

A1 What are the four principal, theoretical determinants of demand?
A2 What is 'effective demand'?
A3 What is 'potential demand'?
A4 What assumptions about the consumer underlie demand theory?
A5 What is the distinction between a movement along the demand curve and a shift of the curve?
A6 Why does the demand for a product increase when price falls?
A7 What are the two types of substitution?
A8 What is joint demand?
A9 Draw income demand curves for (i) a necessity; (ii) a luxury good; (iii) an inferior good.
A10 Define elasticity.
A11 Given a steep demand curve and a shallow curve, which is the more elastic and why?
A12 What is meant by the statement 'the demand for petrol is inelastic?

B. Exercises/Case Studies

B1 A firm processing food found that it could sell 20,000 cans of drink at 25p each. If it reduced the price by 5p, research showed that it would be able to sell 30,000 cans. Calculate the price elasticity of demand. Is the demand elastic? Can you say anything about profit and total revenue resulting from the change in price?

B2 Advertising expenditure for a brand of coffee was raised from £50,000 to £60,000 p.a. During this time sales rose by 25 per cent to a total of 300,000 users. What is the advertising elasticity of demand and how many people used the coffee before the advertising expenditure was increased? Why do you think advertising might have been successful in this case?

B3 As a result of high stocks of unsold cars and a market share of 15 per cent BL cars reduced the price of the Maxi by 10 per cent at the beginning of March 1980. By the end of the month BL's share of the market had risen to 22 per cent and sales of the Maxi were up by 1,500 in February to 4,500 in March. BL cars then announced reductions in the price of the Marina range. The price of the Marina 1300 was cut by £344 to £3,096.
a. What was the price elasticity of demand for Maxis?

b. Assuming a similar elasticity, what percentage increase in sales of Marinas would you expect?

c. Forecasters anticipated a slow down in the sales of cars for 1980. By the end of March this had not materialised. Comment on the likely effects of BL price cuts on the industry as a whole and consider the implications for the market throughout 1980.

B4	Product	Income elasticity of demand	Price elasticity of demand	Promotional elasticity of demand
	A	-1.5	3	0.1
	B	3.0	0.4	2.0
	C	0.9	1.1	0.9

From the above figures, what deductions can you make about the products? What strategies would you propose when deciding on the pricing and image of each of the products?

B5 A deficit on the current account of the balance of payments occurs when the total foreign revenue earned by exports is less than the foreign revenue used to buy imports.

a. Using your knowledge of elasticity, what can you say about the price elasticities of demand for imports and exports if a Government hopes to resolve the deficit by lowering the exchange rate?

b. If imports and exports were both price elastic, what effect would the Government's action have on British industry?

B6 At a meeting of the Car Manufacturers' Association the position of the trade in the previous year was reviewed. Sales were at a new peak of 2 m. cars per annum at an average price of £5,000 per car. However, concern was expressed at the effect of the intensifying recession which made a further increase in the sales unlikely. The trade union representatives present produced evidence that sales would rise to 2.2 m. if the average price of cars was reduced by £100. There was general agreement that such a policy of price cutting would be beneficial. However, one manufacturer disagreed with the trade union figures and presented his own, suggesting that the price elasticity of demand would be 0.5.

a. According to the figures produced by the trade union representatives, what is the elasticity of demand for cars? Show your working.

b. How will the change in price affect profits and revenue?

c. Why do you think the trade union representatives supported this line of action?

d. What would be the effect on total revenue if the elasticity was 0.5?

e. As an individual car manufacturer, explain why you think the information given here would be of limited use in making decisions in your own firm.

C. Essay Questions

C1 How might a knowledge of demand theory help a firm to assess the demand for its products?

C2 How would the reaction of a manufacturer in a highly competitive market differ from one with few competitors when faced with increasing costs of production as a result of inflation?

C3 Discuss how a successful advertising campaign for a branded product could affect the pricing decisions of the manufacturer.

C4 As marketing director of an oil company with excess stocks of petrol, what would you do to try to eliminate them? What reactions would you expect from the market?

C5 'The only way to make the railways profitable is to reduce fares.' Discuss the validity of this statement.

C6 How could a firm use information on price, income and cross elasticities of demand?

Chapter 4

Marketing Information

Objective: *To show the need for marketing information, and the type of information required. To suggest ideas for testing its accuracy, and its use to help forecasting.*

Synopsis: *Firms need to gather information on the markets for their products. On the basis of this information they can evaluate the marketing options, forecast future positions, and begin to develop a strategy for their products. Firms need to be clear what information they want, and should use existing sources whenever possible. The value of the information is measured in terms of its cost and use to the organisation.*

Plan of the chapter:

- **4**.1 Introduction
- **4**.2 Market Research
- **4**.3 Types of Information
- **4**.4 Sources of Survey Information
- **4**.5 The Specific Nature of Market Research
- **4**.6 Market Research and New Products
- **4**.7 The Value of Information
  - **4**.7.1 Sampling
  - **4**.7.2 The Quality of Information
  - **4**.7.3 The Returns on Information
- **4**.8 Forecasting

4.1 Introduction

Marketing decisions influence the profitability of an enterprise. They are based on information, intuition and judgement; but in the increasingly complex world of international markets and major investment programmes, less can be left purely to experience and 'feel' because the cost of wrong decisions is enormous. That cost is measured in the immediate financial terms of company losses. In addition, the **opportunity costs** can have long-term repercussions. Resources used to support a failure could have been employed for a profit-earning project. Missed market opportunities are rarely repeated.

Marketing information does not solve problems but it helps to reduce the risk of failure. It covers the whole range of information on the market, the mix and the performance of products. Experience is valuable because it is based on a general knowledge of marketing situations, but it can be dangerous because no two marketing problems are the same, and solutions to similar situations may not apply in different markets. In addition, because the market changes so fast, decisions that worked last year maybe useless now. Judgement is an essential ingredient in decision taking but it must be based on good information.

In Chapter 3 we looked at the theoretical determinants of demand and the inter-relationship between them. The problem with this analysis is that it is static and the assumptions rarely apply in practice. The theory has little direct use for the product manager because he wants definite, numerate information. However, the general principles are important because they highlight the areas where further research should be undertaken into particular markets and products. Once a manager has accepted that income can influence the sale of his products, he can look at the income levels of his market and the way they are changing. He needs to decide how he should price his product and the quantities that he should make. To answer these questions, he requires specific information about the market and competition. He will want to know how to position his product so that all aspects of the marketing operation contribute to the total sales and profits he can earn. This information is provided by market research. Its purpose is to build up forecasts and help in the construction of the market plan which is the blueprint for actions in the company.

4.2 Market Research

In large organisations the link between the decision takers and the market is distant. Because of the size of their operations, errors can be very expensive. Consequently, resources are deployed to obtain the best information on which to base product and market decisions. Market research narrows the gap between producer and consumer, and increases the chance of successful decisions. It covers the process of information gathering. The American Marketing Association defines it as 'The systematic gathering, recording and analysing of data about problems relating to the marketing of goods and services.'

There is usually a great deal of data within the firm, but it has no value unless it is processed and directed to the correct people. For specific requirements it may be necessary to gather new data which is relevant to the problem, and up to date. Correctly used, market information can reduce both time and waste by providing the best basis for decisions. An information system should enable a continuous process of monitoring performance and analysis of the market to be maintained. It should highlight problems and opportunities, provide information necessary to deal with the situation and communicate it to the departments concerned.

The first stage of market research is to clarify the reasons for undertaking it.

market research

[This involves an examination of the marketing problem and the possible solutions to it.] A small firm cannot suddenly branch out into steel manufacture even if a clear unfulfilled market for steel exists. [By looking at the problem and determining the sort of information necessary to solve it, a clear brief can be set out. This prevents any unnecessary expense involved in obtaining information which is irrelevant. Once the objectives have been established the firm can decide on the type of information required, its accuracy and the frequency of reporting. It should also decide, in advance, the actions it will take based on the information and subsequent analysis. Thus, a firm may want information on competitors' prices each month, and if they vary more than 5 per cent from its own prices action will be taken to narrow the gap.]

4.3 Types of Information

Market information can be classified into a variety of different areas. The brief for market research should lay down the requirements for qualitative and quantitative information. Qualitative information refers to the type of product, the sort of needs that it satisfies, the 'fit' with overall product policy and the image of the firm, the quality and appeal it has for consumers. Often this sets the scene for the quantitative aspects of the market which include the size of the total market, the share of that market held by the firm and the potential for expansion, given the capacity of the firm and the strength of the competition.

There is a great deal of information already available within the organisation, such as the records of sales performance by region, product and sales personnel. Experience with distribution channels and promotion methods is valuable internal information which can be used to help design the mix. Trade and technical journals and published material from independent market research agencies such as Media Expenditure Analysis Limited (MEAL) are sources of external information which may affect the marketing decision. An analysis of the trends in the market can be made by referring to the level of orders over a period of time, and this can be compared to general movements in the market. In addition there are continuous surveys, carried out by market research agencies, such as Nielsen, who run a retail audit. Their findings can be purchased relatively inexpensively and may provide vital information on sales of the company and its competitors. The Government is a major source of information, and, carefully used, it can provide details on population through the census and annual abstract of statistics, income and expenditure levels, housing, manufactured goods, the structure of the retail trade and much more, from its many publications.

Only as a last resort should a firm undertake its own surveys or commission an agency to find out specific information. The cost of questionnaires and surveys is high and they take time to construct and carry out. The use of resources in this way is only justified if the information is important and cannot be obtained from any other source.

4.4 Sources of Survey Information

Survey information can take many forms. Questionnaires and structured interviews require careful thought when they are compiled. The interview, as a two-way communication, allows the interviewer to follow up any unusual response and develop it further. While this may provide useful information and ideas for new products it is more difficult to classify the replies. In addition the interviewer may colour the interpretation of the answers. Questionnaires already structure the kind of responses that can be given and the results can be used more easily. However, respondents may find questions difficult to answer and become frustrated. In designing either questionnaire or interview the purpose for which the information is required must be clear. Questions can be pre-tested to see that they are not offensive or ambiguous; they should also be checked to see if they provide the type of information required. Poor wording may lead to the wrong question being answered. There is always the danger of people giving answers they think the interviewer would like rather than reflecting their real views and actions.

Continuous audits provide another source of information. Consumer audits are used to study what people buy. They may take the form of diaries which are kept by a selected group of consumers noting down everything they have bought. The drawback is that filling in the diary is a nuisance and purchases are often not recorded when they happen. Instead, the diary is completed at the end of the week and then some of the purchases have been forgotten. However, this partial memory does give some indication of brand loyalty because there is a greater likelihood of recording the important purchases in the consumer's mind. The diary is also used to monitor television audiences in conjunction with an electronic device which records the time and channel when the television is switched on.

Occasionally dustbin audits are used. By checking cartons and tins in refuse, an indication of the usage of different products emerges. Although time consuming, this method may produce more reliable results than questionnaires and diaries because it avoids the problem of people saying only what they think they should admit to. In a survey conducted recently in America, people were asked how much beer they drank each week. The results showed an average of two cans per person in a particular area but a dustbin audit showed that empty cans were being discarded at a rate of twelve cans per person.

4.5 The Specific Nature of Market Research

Detailed information is needed on the economy. Governments attempt to control income and expenditure through a range of monetary, fiscal and direct control policies and these can significantly affect the market for a particular product. For example, an electronics firm may be very concerned about Government policies with regard to defence expenditure, manufacturers of luxury goods will monitor changes in income tax and VAT. A change in the exchange rate between different currencies will make overseas markets more, or less, profitable. Changes in the law can have widespread implications for the way a product is marketed. Trends within the market may be accentuated by movements in the standard of living. Market research has to take all this into account.

If the firm is to position its product correctly in the market so that it can achieve maximum sales or profit, it needs to build up a 'consumer profile'. As it discovers more about its consumers, the firm can modify the marketing mix to sell its product in the way customers want. It needs to know who its customers are, the type of people according to sex, age, region and socio-economic class. By gathering information on their habits and tastes the firm can begin to understand what motivates the purchase. It can break up the whole market into segments and direct its efforts to suit the different characteristics. Age and regional differences can be very important in determining how people react to the product image. A firm manufacturing baby foods needs to know what shops mothers use, how they decide between competing brands, how important packaging is and what emphasis is placed on convenience for the mother, and taste for the baby.

Socio-economic class is an important classification. Figure 4.1 shows the grading used by the Joint Industry Committee for National Readership Surveys, and although not the only classification used, it is the most important because media circulation and viewing figures are broken down in that way. A large body of information for the consumer profile is linked to it.

Lastly, further mention should be made of market share and market poten-

Social grade	Social status	Head of household's occupation
A	Upper middle class	Higher managerial, administrative or professional
B	Middle class	Intermediate managerial, administrative or professional
C1	Lower middle class	Supervisory or clerical and junior managerial, administrative or professional
C2	Skilled working class	Skilled manual workers
D	Working class	Semi-skilled and unskilled manual workers
E	Those at lowest levels of subsistance	State pensioners or widows (no other earner), casual or lower grade workers

Fig. 4.1: Socio-Economic Grades (Source: JICNARS)

tial. These two figures are extremely important because they determine much
of subsequent policy. Market share is the proportion of total market sales
accounted for by the firm, while market potential is the sales level that it could
achieve with its present capacity. Actual sales against market share give an
indication of whether the market as a whole is expanding or declining. Dependent on this, the firm will alter its marketing mix to achieve a desired level of
sales. The firm which has the largest market share is known as the market
leader and it usually has more flexibility than the other firms to change the
way a product is marketed. In addition, its market standing describes where
the firm is, in comparison to its competitors.

4.6 Market Research and New Products

Firms rely on new products to take the place of those that have lost their
appeal and been superseded. They present special problems to the firm. There
is no feedback information from which to predict likely sales and product
characteristics. However, market research plays an important part in the process of developing new products. It can highlight gaps in the market by isolating areas where consumer needs are not satisfied. Information on the way
existing products are used, and misused, can show opportunities for new products. Customer complaints may underline problems with the products of the
company and its competitors. This can indicate areas for improvement and
new product development. Segmentation, splitting the potential market into
groups by occupation, income group, age and so on, can suggest new markets
and products. For example, Birds Eye researched the market for fish fingers
and found that it was essentially conservative and concerned with nutritional
value. This information helped to harden the emphasis of its strategy for fish
fingers but it also underlined the opportunities for a new product to meet the
needs of a younger, more adventurous market.

Continuous research can show up opportunities for new products as market
conditions change. For example, the mid 1970s saw cocoa prices rise very
rapidly (166% in 1976). To cushion the impact of higher prices Cadburys, the
market leader, reduced the weight of its Dairy Milk bars. However, market
research carried out by Rowntrees showed that there was now a gap in the
market, and that people felt a thin chocolate bar did not taste as good as a
thick one. This information supported its launch of the Yorkie bar which,
although expensive, returned 'chunky' bars to the market. Within two years
Yorkie held 20 per cent of the chocolate bar market and Cadburys had retali-
ated by changing the shape of its product to a thicker bar.

Once an idea has been established the process of research is much the same
as for existing products. Is the product in line with company policy and is
there sufficient expertise and capacity to move it at a profit-making price? How
large will the market be and how is it likely to change with new conditions?
What is the market like and how does the consumer work? What price and

promotional policies are going to lead to the greatest customer satisfaction and hence larger sales? What are the key product attributes that are important to the customer?

Example: A firm manufacturing garden furniture is considering widening its range of products. It has been considering the possibility of manufacturing greenhouses. This would be in line with its general product range and it already uses wood, glass and steel in its chairs and tables. The first task is to discover more about the market, and the existing greenhouses available. Some of this information will come from the stores that sell its furniture as well as greenhouses made by other firms. The firm can sound out the trade reaction to a new greenhouse and discover which designs sell well and at what price. There may be additional information from past consumer reports published by Which?. *This will give an indication of the attributes that are important to users and the strengths and weaknesses of competitors' models. Advice may be sought from gardeners' associations, professional bodies such as the Royal Horticultural Society and the informed opinion of experts. A survey of gardeners may be carried out. Trends in the market will be examined to assess the chance of success.*

The information from these sources is then analysed to provide a list of the key requirements of a greenhouse from the consumer's viewpoint. These might include design (lean-to or self-contained), size, materials (steel or wood frame), colour of frame, accessories such as trays and automatic ventilation, and durability and strength. At this stage a decision has to be taken over the importance of each of these and a compromise is made to give the best 'fit' with the market. A mock-up may be constructed and tested with a group of consumers. At the same time, the firm will gather information on whether to sell the greenhouse in kit form for the gardener to assemble himself, or as a complete package delivered and assembled by the distributor. Different advertisements may be tested to see what form they should take: direct selling off the page through mail order, or display advertising to persuade the consumer to buy from a shop, the copy *that will create the strongest demand. If the greenhouse is to be put together by the customer the firm will test how professional the assembled greenhouse looks, and the ease of constructing it. The consumer panel will be asked about price ranges at which they would buy the product in the light of their perception of its value and competitors' prices.*

Based on this information the firm will decide whether or not to go ahead with manufacturing the greenhouse, possibly testing it in a limited market before launching nationally. Figure 4.2 shows a schematic approach that the firm might take.

4.7 The Value of Information

When a firm decides to gather information, it has to balance the quality of the information against the cost of obtaining it. Quality depends on the source, the

Information type	Information source

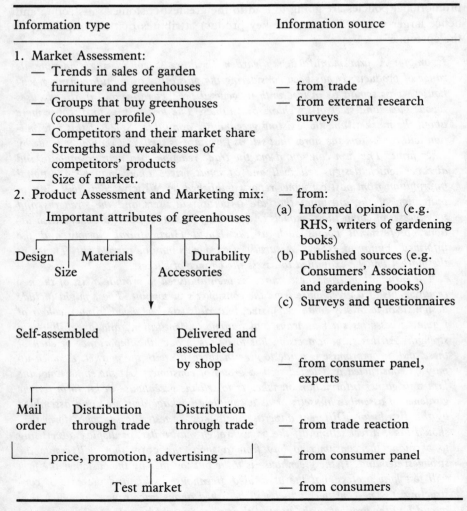

1. Market Assessment:
   — Trends in sales of garden
     furniture and greenhouses   — from trade
   — Groups that buy greenhouses   — from external research
     (consumer profile)   surveys
   — Competitors and their market share
   — Strengths and weaknesses of
     competitors' products
   — Size of market.
2. Product Assessment and Marketing mix: — from:
       Important attributes of greenhouses   (a) Informed opinion (e.g.
     RHS, writers of gardening
     books)

Design   Materials   Durability   (b) Published sources (e.g.
     Size   Accessories   Consumers' Association
     and gardening books)
       (c) Surveys and questionnaires

Self-assembled   Delivered and
       assembled
       by shop   — from consumer panel,
       experts

Mail   Distribution   Distribution
order   through trade   through trade   — from trade reaction

   price, promotion, advertising   — from consumer panel

    Test market   — from consumers

Fig. 4.2: Framework for market information on the launch of a greenhouse

size of the sample taken and the way it is constructed. Value depends on its
use, accuracy and the cost and time taken to obtain it. Sampling is a means of
finding out about the market without interviewing everyone within it.

4.7.1 Sampling

Surveys are carried out to discover specific information not available from any
existing source. Obviously, in a mass market it is impossible to ask every
potential or actual consumer what they think of a product or how they make
their purchasing decisions. Survey work is based on sampling. A representative proportion, or sample, of the total market is approached. For the informa-

tion to be of any use it is essential that the sample accurately reflects the 'population' from which it is taken. Samples fall into three types:

1. *Random sample*, where everyone has an equal chance of being asked. In most cases this will be too broad because the product may not be relevant to people asked.
2. *Stratified sample*, where particular groups of the population are chosen. Thus a firm manufacturing perfume might take a group of women between twenty-five and thirty-five years.
3. *Quota sample*, where the group taken reflects certain characteristics known to exist in the market. If an analysis of customers using a supermarket showed that the ratio of women to men was five to one, the quota sample would be constructed to a similar ratio.

Both stratified and quota samples can be random within their groups. Most market research uses the random quota sample because of its relative cheapness, but great care has to be taken in its construction to ensure that there is no bias; for example, where one group within the sample is over-represented.

4.7.2 The Quality of Information

The size of the sample depends on the accuracy required. Inevitably if we do not question everyone there is a chance that the results will not be a 100 per cent accurate reflection of the relevant population. However, most market research information does not have to be totally accurate. If a firm wants to know its market share, it will not matter whether the figure is 25 per cent or 26 per cent, but it will be important to discover whether it is 25 per cent or 50 per cent.

Suppose a firm producing after-shave wants to know what proportion of a group of 100,000 men use its brand. It could discover this by asking everyone in the group. However, this would be both expensive and time consuming. It would also be unnecessary. Provided a representative sample was taken the proportion of the sample using the brand should reflect the proportion in the group. However, it is possible that the sample is not a true reflection of the group.

Suppose that 20,000 out of the group of 100,000 actually used the firm's after-shave. Usership would be 20 per cent and so a sample of 1,000 men from the group might include 200 users. However, it would not be very surprising if there were 195 men who used the after-shave. It would be odd if only four men in the sample used the product. That finding would suggest either that the sample was not representative, or that usership in the whole group was really well below 20 per cent. It would not be conclusive proof because it is just possible that the sample was a freak occurrence. It would simply be very unlikely. So what variations from 20 per cent could reasonably be expected to occur?

If a large number of samples of 1,000 men were taken and the number of users in each sample noted down, the resultant frequency curve would look like the one in Fig. 4.3.

Frequency

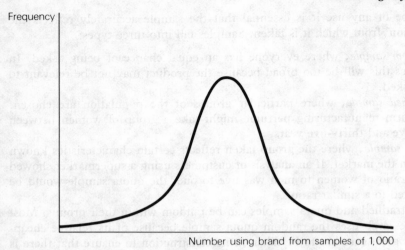

Number using brand from samples of 1,000

Fig. 4.3: The normal distribution

This curve is known as a normal distribution curve. It has certain properties:

- The area under the curve is proportional to the total number of samples taken.
- The curve is symmetric about the **mean, mode** and **median**.
- The spread of values about the mean is a function of the standard deviation (σ) of the values.

In fact, 68 per cent of all observations lie within one standard deviation of the mean, 95.4 per cent within two standard deviations and 99.8 per cent within three standard deviations as shown in Fig. 4.4.

Frequency

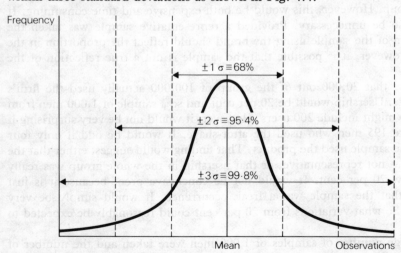

$\pm 1\,\sigma \equiv 68\%$

$\pm 2\,\sigma \equiv 95 \cdot 4\%$

$\pm 3\,\sigma \equiv 99 \cdot 8\%$

Mean   Observations

Fig. 4.4: The standard deviation

Thus it is 99.8 per cent certain that the sample will give results which lie within three standard deviations each side of the mean.

If we know the mean and standard deviation of the sample we can check its accuracy. These can be calculated from formulae.

mean $\quad = \text{n} \times \text{p}$

$\sigma \quad = \sqrt{\text{n} \times \text{p} \times \text{q}}$

Where n $\quad$ = number in sample

p $\quad$ = probability of a particular outcome occurring

q $\quad$ = probability of outcome not occurring.

In this case the sample size (n) is 1,000

p $\quad$ = $\quad$ probability of a man using the brand $\quad \dfrac{200}{1,000} = 0.2$

q $\quad$ = $\quad$ probability of a man not using the brand $\quad \dfrac{800}{1,000} = 0.8$

So the mean n.p. $= 1,000 \times 0.2 = 200$

and the standard deviation $\sqrt{\text{n.p.q.}} = \sqrt{1,000 \times 0.8 \times 0.2} \simeq 13$

Thus we could be 95 per cent certain that our sample would yield a number of users that lay between two standard deviations on either side of the mean. This would be $200 \pm (13 \times 2) = 174$ to 226 men. By taking larger samples the accuracy can be increased.

A sample of 10,000 would give a range of 1,920 to 2,080 men.

4.7.3 The Returns on Information

Whenever any research is undertaken the cost involved must be balanced against the benefits resulting from the findings. Obviously judgement is necessary, but decision tree analysis provides a means of putting a value on information. Consider the following hypothetical example. A small engineering firm is considering whether to introduce a new product. Market forecasts suggest that there will be a 75 per cent chance of success in the launch and the firm has to decide whether to manufacture the product itself or subcontract production. Figure 4.5 summarises the estimates of returns.

	Success 75%	*Failure 25%*
Manufacture	+ £500,000	– £600,000
Subcontract	+ £200,000	– £160,000
Do nothing	£0	£0

Fig. 4.5: Estimate of returns for each alternative

At this stage a decision tree can be constructed to indicate the course of action. Expected values are calculated by multiplying the actual values by probability of that outcome (see Fig. 4.6).

From Fig. 4.7 the firm will go ahead and manufacture the product itself. However, it may be reluctant to risk losing £600,000. Now assume that the firm can research the market and obtain perfect information on whether the

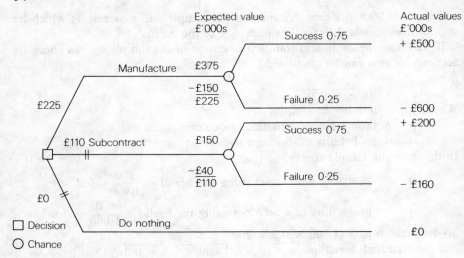

Fig. 4.6: The decision tree

product will be a success at a cost of £100,000. Would this information be worth its cost?

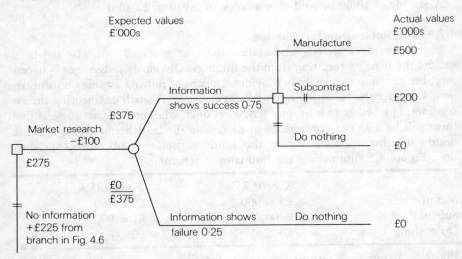

Fig. 4.7: The decision tree, including market information

This decision tree shows that on balance it would be worth doing the research since the outcome is £50,000 greater. The actual outcome will be +£400,000 if the research shows that the project will be successful and a loss of £100,000 if it fails. The maximum value of perfect information in this case would be £150,000 since the outcomes with or without research would be the same. Since no information is perfect, its actual value is rather less. The decision tree would be further complicated by applying probability to the accuracy of the forecasts.

4.8 Forecasting

Market research is designed to build up a picture of the market and the forces that operate on it. From this the firm can alter its product and marketing mix if necessary. It is also the basis of forecasting the volume and value of sales and through them the profitability of the firm. Predicting what will happen in the future is not easy and there is no guarantee that forecasts will be proved right. However, the value of forecasting lies in focusing attention on the factors that influence sales and producing a definite set of expectations in the form of a plan.

For as full a picture as possible long- and short-term forecasts are needed, although the accuracy of short-term forecasts is greater because fewer variables can change.

Research findings and the informed judgement of management are backed up by mathematical techniques used to relate different variables and highlight trends from past information. Time-series analysis refers to the range of techniques which produce underlying trends. The **method of moving averages** also isolates random **cyclical** and **seasonal variations** from the trend. For example, from past sales figures, once the **trend** has been drawn out into the future it can be overlaid with seasonal variations to give the expected sales figure for each season. **Correlation analysis** is used to discover the extent of the link between variables such as advertising expenditure and sales so that estimates of future sales can be made based on advertising expenditure. As with time series analysis, there is no guarantee that the relationships will remain constant or that past variations will be repeated.

The uncertainty of forecasting means that several different methods should be used. By combining the results a realistic range of estimates can be made. However, assumptions will be involved which may prove wrong in the event. The dramatic rise in oil prices in 1974 meant that forecasts of energy consumption and growth were widely out. Whether the timing of the price rises could have been predicted is open to question, but the fact is that it was not included in the forecasts. It does illustrate the need to make allowances for likely movements of all the factors affecting markets including technical change, competitors' actions and the general economic position.

Work Section

A. Revision Questions

A1 Define market research.

A2 Why is market research so important, especially for large companies?

A3 What should a market information system do?

A4 What types of information are there?

A5 What kind of information is available from the Government?

A6 Why should the firm use questionnaires and surveys only as a last resort?

A7 What is a consumer profile?

A8 What are the three types of sample?

A9 What are the properties of a normal distribution curve?

A10 What is the purpose of forecasting?

B. Exercises/Case Studies

B1 In an imaginary situation, the Post Office carried out a survey to check the speed of first class letter post. 5,000 letters were sent out with a reply-paid card for people to note the date of arrival. To eliminate bias, the sample reflected the usual traffic of letters between centres of population. The bulk of the mail is within, and between, towns, with a small proportion of rural letters and letters between rural areas and towns. This information came from internal Post Office records. In addition the sample matched the proportion of socio-economic groups in the country.

At the same time the consumer pressure group (The Post Office Users Council) sent out 1,000 letters to its members asking them to send three letters to other members and to keep a note of all deliveries of first class mail in the following fortnight. They could calculate the time taken for delivery by checking the arrival date against the postmark.

The results of both surveys are set out below:

Post Office Socio-economic group of respondent	Replies (%)	Post Office Users Council Socio-economic group of respondent	Replies (%)
A, B	22	A, B	60
C_1, C_2	48	C_1, C_2	30
D, E	30	D, E	10
	——		——
	100		100

No. in survey: 5,000   No. of letters recorded: 8,600
Replies   : 3,800

Time taken for delivery (% of replies)

Post Office		Post Office Users Council	
1 Day	95	1 Day	74
2 Days	3	2 Days	20
More than 2 Days	2	More than 2 Days	6
	100		100

Questions:
a. What information is available from secondary sources?
b. How would you explain the differences in the results?

B2 The managing director of a company manufacturing washing up liquid is concerned about the familiarity of the market with its brand name 'Ozo'. If less than 70 per cent of all consumers recognise the name, he thinks he should launch a major TV advertising campaign.

The market research department of the company selects a random sample of 200 consumers and asks them: 'With what do you associate the name "Ozo"?' 144 consumers correctly identify the name.

a. Discuss whether the managing director should be satisfied with the result, justifying your answers in words and figures.
b. The market research department repeats the survey, this time with a larger sample of 1,000 consumers. How many would have to recognise the name in order to provide satisfactory evidence that no major advertising campaign is necessary?
c. Comment on the question asked by the market research department. How does it affect your answers to (a) and (b)?

(For a normal probability model with the parameters p, q, n, the standard deviation is given by the formula $\sqrt{n.p.q.}$)

(Cambridge Local Examinations Syndicate, 1974.1.4)

B3 A company is considering whether to introduce a new product. It will only launch it after it has seen the findings of a test market. The cost of running the test market is £200,000. Estimates suggest that the chance the test market will show a strong demand is 0.5, a satisfactory demand 0.3, and a weak demand 0.2. To support the launch, if the demand is strong the company will undertake a major marketing campaign, (A), which will cost £500,000; if the demand is satisfactory it will undertake a modest campaign, (B), costing £200,000; and if the demand is weak the product will be dropped. The table shows the revenues from each project and the probabilities of success or failure.

Campaign A			Campaign B	
Probability		Revenue (£)	Probability	Revenue (£)
Success	0.8	2m.	0.9	1m.
Failure	0.2	– 1m.	0.1	– 0.5m.

Should the company go ahead with the test market?

B4 The table below shows sales figures of a large clothing manufacturer in an index series based on the third quarter of 1975.

a. Calculate the trend figures by moving average, assuming a four quarter seasonal cycle, and project the trend figures to the second quarter of 1978.

b. Identify the seasonal variation pattern, and calculate the projected figure for the first quarter of 1978.

Note: Work to the nearest whole unit of the index series.

Quarters	I	II	III	IV
1974	95	79	88	85
1975	91	95	100	95
1976	119	110	105	99
1977	115	110	117	109

(Cambridge Local Examinations Syndicate, 1978.1.3)

C. Essay Questions

C1 How should a firm organise its market research?

C2 Comment on the view that conditions in the market change so fast that it is a waste of time gathering information and forecasting.

C3 A firm manufacturing industrial machinery is considering adding a new lathe to its product range. Suggest a plan for its market research.

C4 Should a firm contract all its market research to an independent, outside agency?

Chapter 5

Product Policy and Planning

Objective: *To show the importance of examining the product range and developing new items as old ones decline. To explain the concept of the product life cycle and its use as a planning tool. To develop a broad market plan linked to marketing objectives.*

Synopsis: *An analysis of product performance and the creation of a marketing strategy is essential if a firm is to secure its future. New products are the lifeblood of an explanding organisation and the concept of the product life cycle can help firms to plan their marketing strategy. The market plan provides a framework for product development and the basis for decisions on the marketing mix.*

Plan of the chapter:

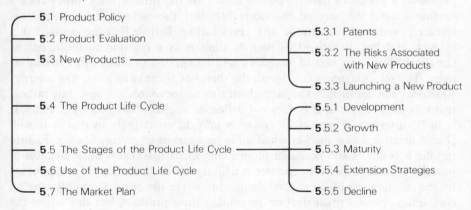

- **5**.1 Product Policy
- **5**.2 Product Evaluation
- **5**.3 New Products
  - **5**.3.1 Patents
  - **5**.3.2 The Risks Associated with New Products
  - **5**.3.3 Launching a New Product
- **5**.4 The Product Life Cycle
- **5**.5 The Stages of the Product Life Cycle
  - **5**.5.1 Development
  - **5**.5.2 Growth
  - **5**.5.3 Maturity
  - **5**.5.4 Extension Strategies
  - **5**.5.5 Decline
- **5**.6 Use of the Product Life Cycle
- **5**.7 The Market Plan

5.1 Product Policy

All firms rely on the sales of their products to produce sufficient revenue to create a profit, although nationalised industries are given differing objectives by the Government of the day. Firms vary in the size of profits that they want, but in all cases the product or service is the lifeblood of the organisation and must be constantly reviewed to ensure that it is contributing enough. To do this, firms have to examine how well each of their products fits consumers' needs, the nature and extent of the competition and the changing market and product trends which are likely to affect future sales. All products eventually go into decline – some sooner than others – and this creates an emphasis on new products to replace those which are fading, so that the profitability of the whole enterprise can be maintained. Hence there is a constant need for product evaluation.

5.2 Product Evaluation

Organisations must be aware of the market that they are in, and often this awareness is limited by existing output reflecting product, rather than market-orientation. For example, orginally Black and Decker was solely involved in industrial power tools. However, because of competition and market saturation it re-examined its product and decided to apply its skills to the 'do-it-yourself' market. Having re-defined its market, new avenues opened with home workshop tools and powered gardening accessories.

The market should be looked at in as broad a way as possible to enable the firm to react in advance of changed conditions, especially those which are likely to cause a decline in a market. The decline of the railways reflects the view that successive managements were concerned with trains, rather than providing a means of moving people about. At the turn of the century such a decline must have seemed inconceivable, but the railways had themselves replaced canal and road traffic fifty years earlier. British Rail has realised this in part, and has diversified further into hotels as a reaction to the needs of travellers. The same sort of analysis could be applied to many other organisations. The oil industry is faced with the threat of alternative sources of energy. This does not mean that the oil industry must inevitably collapse but rather, that it is likely to suffer if it does not define its market widely enough. Thus, it is in its interests to undertake research into different fuels so that it is well placed to meet a new market when oil is replaced as an energy source. Failure to take account of the potential movements in its markets is an indication of product-orientation where expertise in drilling for, and refining, oil is supported by the creation of sufficient final demand to cover the costs. Certainly, the oil companies spend a great deal on promoting their product, but this is not the same as being market-oriented. Selling oil is essential for the continuation of exploration and refining, and the oil companies have invested very heavily in the plant necessary to do this. They have spent less time discovering what it is that consumers really want. Oil derivatives are unpleasant: consider the nuisance and smell of a large central heating oil tank or the inconvenience of continually stopping to fill up the petrol tank of your car. Consumers put up with this not because they want to buy oil, but because they wish to be warm, or to travel. Selling is concerned with persuading people to buy more of a product – marketing includes this – but it also involves reacting to consumer wants.

Just as there are dangers in defining a product and market too narrowly, diversification can create difficulties in the form of over-stretched resources. However, failure to take note of changing events is a guaranteed way to allow an industry to run down.

An example of the reaction to altered circumstances is the diversification of the tobacco companies into non-related areas, such as foodstuffs, in the wake of mounting evidence of the dangers of smoking. Many of the basic market characteristics are the same and the tobacco companies were well placed to use their marketing knowledge in new mass consumption areas. Thus they could employ their own specific strengths in new areas, giving themselves a broader base from which to operate.

It is also essential to consider the state of competition in the market. Much can be learnt about the market from the performance of similar products, and the findings included in the development of a new product. When Guccione started up *Penthouse* in 1965 he had analysed the major competitor as *Playboy* and this meant that, if he was to succeed, his magazine would have to embrace certain of the *Playboy* characteristics, and improve on them. Thus, although he was engaged in a new venture, his broad objectives were governed by the product he was trying to overtake. Even the pricing decision was governed by *Playboy*'s newstand price. What Guccione was trying to do was to fill a perceived market more effectively than the existing competition by altering the content to suit that market.

Product evaluation involves an examination into the need the product serves, its customers and what is special about them, its differences from other products on the market and how it fits within the company's product range. By looking at products critically the firm can rationalise its range so that no two items are competing with each other, and ensure that there is sufficient distinctiveness to create brand awareness.

5.3 New Products

Production evaluation shows the firm how its product is placed in the market. It is part of the process of building up an overall product policy which will determine the firm's future. A coherent policy of adding to, and deleting from, the product range enables firms to plan ahead. This has led to an increased interest in new products and the problems of their introduction. Since technical innovation is so rapid, the life of products in their original form has become much shorter. Hence the need to generate new ideas for future cash earners. Indeed it may be that firms can only grow if they are prepared to innovate and develop new products and markets.

Product evaluation provides one way of developing new products as natural extensions to existing ones. A company wishing to diversify into new, but related, areas can analyse the strengths and weaknesses of its product line and the way it is handled. From this, a particular strength or '**distinctive compe-**

tence' can emerge which will give a direction to the development of new ideas. For example, Bic pioneered the disposable Biro and used its 'distinctive competence' of inexpensive throw-away products when it launched the disposable razor.

5.3.1 **Patents**

When a firm (or an individual) invents a new product or manufacturing process it usually wants to prevent competitors from imitating the development and exploiting it commercially. The patent system is designed to give the innovator that protection in return for publication of the details of the idea.

The granting of 'letters patent' gives the innovator the sole right to make, use and sell the invention for a limited time. However, in order to gain that right the inventor must provide the Patent Office with enough information to enable 'anyone skilled in the art concerned' to understand what is involved in the invention. The objectives of the patent system are twofold. By granting a 'monopoly' right the inventor is given the opportunity to produce and sell the idea without a competitor undercutting his price. In this way, the inventor should be able to recover his research costs, and the protection acts as an incentive for product innovations. The other side of the bargain is the provision of information, so that anyone wanting to undertake research has access to the ideas that have already been developed.

To justify the cost of applying for a patent the firm must be ready to develop the product or process commercially, and the success of the product is dependent on the marketing and production skills of the firm. Alternatively, the firm may allow another enterprise to use the invention 'under licence', receiving a royalty for each item sold. Failure to exploit the invention can lead to the monopoly right being withdrawn. The patent renewal fees, payable every year after the first four years, become more expensive, to encourage production. Except in certain cases where the patent technique has no commercial possibilities because it is too technically advanced, the maximum life of a patent is twenty years.

The procedure for obtaining a patent involves the provision of a detailed specification of the product or process. To qualify for a patent the invention must be new and not produced elsewhere. There then follows an exhaustive examination to check the invention and ensure that there are no precedents for it. The patent is published eighteen months after application and finally sealed some time after this. The gap allows time for objections to be lodged with the Patent Office.

In addition to patents, other forms of protection exist in different areas. Registered trademarks and designs are taken by manufacturers to protect the reputation and design of their products. Copyright exists to protect authors, artists and musicians from copying by unauthorised people. Unlike the other forms of protection, copyright is only breached if the material has been published and therefore available to be copied.

5.3.2 **The Risks Associated with New Products**

Established firms with their own research departments are usually better able to generate new products because of their expertise within existing markets. However, launching new products is notoriously risky. A recent report showed that of 400 new food products launched in 1965 only 20 per cent were still available ten years later, with most being withdrawn in the early years after the launch. In 1966 a Nielsen analysis showed that 54 per cent of new products never went beyond a test market. Figure 5.1 shows the fortunes of a group of new food products launched in 1969. The sharp drop in the first two years reflects the failure of products in their test markets. After four years products which have not met profit or sales objectives are withdrawn.

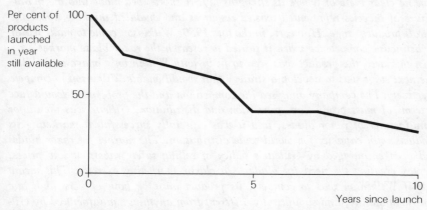

(*Source*: 'New Products: How to succeed when the odds are against you', by John Madell, *Marketing Week*; 22.2.80)

Fig. 5.1: The success of new products

The high failure rate and the costs of launching a new product mean that there is a temptation to leave others to break new ground and follow in as quickly as possible once the idea has been shown to work. However, one of the largest categories of failures is the '**me-too**', or imitation product. Brand loyalties are often well established in the early years of a product's life.

5.3.3 Launching a New Product

Usually it is the large companies with high market shares who are the 'market innovators' because new ideas are important for them to retain their position. Their ability to deal with new ideas is limited by the extent to which they have already committed themselves to existing production, and their requirement to obtain a reasonable return on their initial investment. This can act against them if a smaller company can achieve sufficient output of a new product. Gillette was faced with precisely this problem when Wilkinson introduced its stainless steel razor blade in 1961. It is worth examining this situation further because it highlights several aspects of product policy working within practical constraints.

Example: The introduction of the stainless steel razor blade. Wilkinson had made its name for quality manufacture of swords, and this meant that it faced alternating periods of prosperity and depression depending on the political state of the nation. During the First World War it manufactured 2½m. bayonets and its maximum capacity of swords, but in the ensuing peace the company found itself without a market. As such, this reflected a short-sighted outlook on the part of the company, and although Wilkinson diversified into garden equipment which used its distinctive competence of manufacturing 'sharp cutting edges' it appeared to have no clear view of where its strengths lay. A short-lived move into the manufacture of bicycles represented wasted resources and muddled thinking about the overall product range. However, in the late 1950s Wilkinson came to make use of its distinctive competence when it started to research the razor blade market.

In this area the product was seen to fit in with Wilkinson's image and skills. The next stage was to develop a strategy that would enable Wilkinson to compete effectively. The company analysed the competition and the problems it would face in terms of mass production, promotion and distribution. Gillette was the major manufacturer of razor blades, and it was especially successful at marketing its products with capacity for world-wide distribution. The market for razor blades had been encouraged by Gillette's policy of selling safety razors at low prices, thereby creating the need for blades – a classic marketing exercise. This meant that if Wilkinson was to compete, its product must be both of very high and consistent quality, and significantly different from anything manufactured by Gillette. These conditions created problems for Wilkinson with no experience of mass production or large-scale marketing, and any decision on how to exploit the product development (stainless steel, long-lasting blade) had to take this into account.

The smallness of Wilkinson relative to Gillette meant that it could have aimed for low output and restricted markets, posing no real threat to Gillette, and expanded slowly as funds were generated and marketing expertise developed. This policy could have worked in one of two ways. Firstly, by remaining small, Gillette might well have ignored the incursion into its market, and Wilkinson could have allowed its superior blade to sell itself on quality grounds, so avoiding considerable market expenses. Secondly, Gillette could have taken time and used the product development to introduce a similar blade when it fitted its production schedule. It could then use its superior production and marketing ability to oust Wilkinson.

The alternative strategy for Wilkinson was to build up production capacity and break into the market, risking Gillette's possible counter attack. By choosing this course, some response was inevitable and Wilkinson would have to rely on Gillette taking some time to change its product line. Gillette had just launched the 'Blue Gillette' blade and it was likely that it would have to let that run for a while to recoup development and production costs. In the event, that is what happened. Gillette was constrained by internal policy and, quite reasonably, decided to see what was going to happen with the Wilkinson development. It was quite likely that Wilkinson would run into problems of production and quality control, but at the same time provide useful information on market reaction to the stainless blade and its higher price relative to other blades.

The Wilkinson launch in 1961 was very successful, and shortages of production capacity immediately occurred. Expansion increased by 100 per cent in the following year, and again by 300 per cent in 1963. Its market share rose to 34 per cent and by the time Gillette produced its 'Silver Gillette' blade, Wilkinson was a major competitor. However, Wilkinson was forced to react to Gillette by reducing prices.

In the subsequent period Wilkinson has maintained a large share of the market which, as a whole, has had to face intense competition from electric razors. A number of 'extension strategies' have followed, using the closeness of a wet shave as the prime selling point. New single-edged blades with dispenser packs, the development of disposable razors and the two-blade cartridges have all been employed to increase sales, and extend the life of the wet razor.

Product policy is illustrated in the Wilkinson–Gillette example. Firstly, the determination of a distinctive competence, which gives the firm its direction, and some 'feel' for the possible product areas it can enter. Secondly, product evaluation, to see how existing products fit with consumer needs as perceived by the firm. Thirdly, an examination of the competition to determine competitor strengths and future product developments. Fourthly, an analysis of the constraints operating on the firm limiting the scope of its action; and fifthly, a continuous evaluation of likely changes in the market which enable the firm to anticipate moves by competitors and develop new products to maintain market leadership. This leads to a discussion of the product life cycle and its use in developing product policy.

5.4 The Product Life Cycle

Just as humans have a particular life cycle which in broad terms can be predicted, going from childhood to old age, so products follow a similar route. The 'life' of a product varies in length, some reaching a plateau of sales where they stay for long periods – Bovril, for example – and some following a dramatic rise and then rapidly fading away, such as high fashion clothing. Dress hemlines represent a familiar styling change going up and down like yo-yos from year to year. In the more staid men's fashion market, lapels on jackets change from narrow to broad, although the transitions seem to take longer. There is also that group of products which go through phases and then fade away completely – klacker balls, hoola hoops and skateboards experienced short-lived high sales and then largely disappeared from the market.

Observations of the fortunes of products have led to the concept of the product life cycle and a typical path is shown in Figure 5.2.

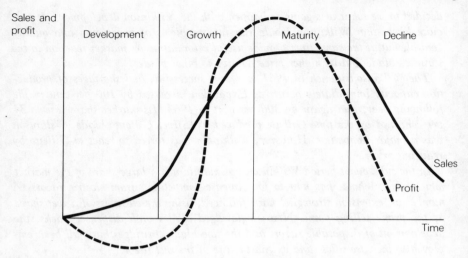

Fig. 5.2: The product life cycle

All products follow this four-stage cycle but the length of each phase varies depending on the nature of the product, the marketing policies adopted and the changes in technology, competition and law. No two products have identical life cycles and marketing decisions must be taken in the light of the particular characteristics of the product and market. Slavishly following a predetermined cycle leads to all sorts of problems, either because a product is wrongly thought to have reached the decline stage and is consequently removed from the market (so killing a potentially lucrative profit earner), or because it is felt that a product should have a longer maturity. Continued marketing support is then used to maintain something that has been superseded and is declining.

The existence of a product life cycle enables firms to plan their overall product line. Ideally, they would like to arrange their product portfolio in such a way that some products in their range are passing through different stages at the same time. In this way a firm can prevent the situation of all its major profit earners entering the decline stage together, so putting the whole enterprise into jeopardy. By protecting their cash flow, firms can maintain a position of financial strength from which to innovate and develop new products. Knowledge of a product's position on the cycle also has clear implications for the most suitable marketing strategy. It helps determine what type of promotion is required, when extension strategies should be introduced and when and how a product should be removed from the market. If a firm has some idea of how the product stands and its likely profile, it can plan its marketing effort in advance so that it is well placed to react to changing market conditions. It can also decide, in advance, when to delete the product from its range. In spite of the difficulties of forecasting and of discovering exactly where the product lies in its cycle, planning for change will always put the firm at an advantage.

5.5 The Stages of the Product Life Cycle

5.5.1 Development

For the early part of this stage the product is still in its research phase, both in terms of product research (developing new materials and methods of manufacture) and market research (finding out how consumers are likely to react to the final result and how it should be presented to the market). The costs of research are very high, and since only limited production runs are likely profits are low. Many products fail to get past this stage either because they are found not to have the anticipated market, or because the costs of the launch are too great for the limited financial and manpower resources of the firm. The process of creating new markets and gaining consumer acceptance is complicated and costly, and it is often difficult to persuade managers that they should release resources from successful, but declining, products for the benefit of new, untried ones.

As part of the overall research, many firms use test markets in selected regions to see how consumers react to the product. This provides information on consumer attitudes, and on how the product may best be distributed, packaged and promoted. Since the test market occurs before the full launch it may provide valuable advance warning of changes in the stages of the cycle nationally, so that the firm can prepare for them. The test market run should also highlight any production problems. The test market may be expensive, but if the product does not perform well, it enables the firm to alter aspects of the mix, or to drop the product, before the cost of a national launch and full-scale promotion is incurred. However, a test market may provide competitors with useful insight into product development and so lose the firm some of the advantage of surprise when the product becomes fully available. There is also the danger that the test market may not reflect the characteristics of the country as a whole, and the results can be misleading.

Once the test market findings are available the firm can modify the product or strategy before it goes ahead with the full launch. At this stage there is no real competition. Distribution is selective, with a few outlets most suited to deal with the new product being chosen. Some support will be given to persuade distributors of the value of the product and expected strength of the market.

The actual shape of the development stage is affected by the newness and complexity of the product. If the product is completely new to the market, its development is likely to take longer, and resources will be needed to promote the idea. Thus, when automatic washing machines were introduced it was necessary to underline the problems of existing 'twin tub' machines, and the benefits of a single drum automatic machine which needed less attention. Consumers had to have sufficient time to appreciate their need for the product. One of the reasons for the failure of quadrophonic sound was the difficulty of persuading the market that 'all-round-sound' represented a major improvement. A complex piece of equipment also takes longer to establish because of fear on the part of consumers. Firms need to consider carefully how they present the product so that people feel that they will be able to use it. For example, in one series of commercials for a major washing machine manufacturer the central theme was that of reliability with simplicity, avoiding the servicing problems associated with gimmicks and apparently sophisticated electronics.

5.5.2 Growth

Once the market has accepted the product, sales begin to rise. This calls for a change in marketing strategy since it is necessary to supply a wider market. If advertising has been widespread so that there is considerable consumer awareness, it becomes easier to persuade retailers and wholesalers to stock the product. Some help may be given by the company by providing display units, extending credit to stockists and allowing special trade discounts. Prices may remain reasonably high to recoup some of the development costs and take advantage of the mass market before competitors come in. At this stage, producer sales are likely to exceed actual final sales while distribution channels build up their stocks. Incentives given to distributors depend on the strength of demand and their readiness to take on a new product which will use more of their limited shelf space.

With high sales and prices during this stage, profits rise sharply and because of this there is greater incentive for new companies to enter the market. Competitors have the advantage of entering the market after all the research and development has been completed and financed by the originator. Where research and development costs are high, more firms are likely to hold back and allow another to underwrite the project. Once the originator has shown the pattern of the market, competitors can come in with modified products which have the teething troubles ironed out. They can make alterations where experience has highlighted design faults, and take advantage of any developments in production techniques that reduce unit costs. Since their costs have been less, they may be in a better position to undercut prices. Careful judgement is required here because any new entrant into the market wants to get in as early as possible, while the market is growing and there is room for other manufacturers. Against the apparent advantage of coming in second is the strength of the innovator who may have built up a degree of brand loyalty, and also gathered the pick of the distributors. Once entrenched, competitors have to make a strong case to persuade wholesalers and retailers to stock their product. The outcome is dependent on the relative strengths of the two products and the likely market acceptance of the new one compared to the existing one.

An alternative pricing decision might be made by the originator in an attempt to discourage competition, by pricing the product more cheaply, thus reducing profits. This has the effect of making the market less attractive to enter and enlarging the potential sales by increasing the mass-market opportunities. However, it extends the payback period for development costs.

During the growth stage, marketing strategies are likely to change. The problem is no longer one of persuading the market to try the product, but rather to use a particular brand. Thus advertising moves towards brand identification and awareness, with the special characteristics of a particular brand being emphasised. There may be special offers, concessions to stockists and professional help in setting up store displays in an attempt to keep the consumer and the trade favourably disposed to the product.

5.5.3 Maturity

Eventually, the market becomes saturated when household demand has been satisfied and distribution channels are full. Sales level off, and over-capacity in production becomes apparent. As soon as this happens, competition intensifies since each manufacturer wants to ensure that he can maintain production at a level which gives him low unit costs. The greater the costs of production and the initial investment, the more important it is to maintain a high output so that the fixed overheads can be spread over a large number of goods. Figure 5.3 shows a simplified break-even chart. With high overheads, the break-even output occurs at high levels of output. There is increased pressure to reduce costs (although marketing costs may rise to keep the product at the front of consumer awareness), and also to reduce prices to stave off competitors. The effect of lowering prices is to reduce the gradient of the sales revenue curve, so increasing the break-even output.

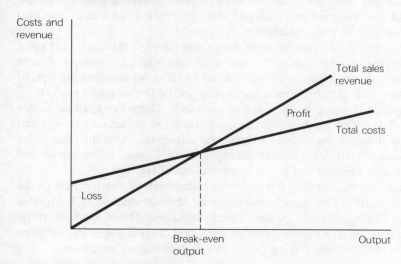

Fig. 5.3: Break-even chart

At this stage retail outlets play an increasing part since it is essential to retain their loyalty. They become active in the selling process, and more assistance is given in display. Distributor margins are increased so that sufficient shelf space is supplied and more is spent advertising the brand, thus supporting the retailer's decision to continue to stock it. The nature of advertising changes, emphasising further the differences between one brand and its competitors. Weaker rivals begin to disappear and the market is left to the larger manufacturers.

5.5.4 Extension strategies

Firms try to retain their market share by employing 'extension strategies' which may involve modification of the product in the light of technical improvement – 'new improved powered steering' or the development of new styling creating 'appearance obsolescence' and cashing in on the desire for 'this year's model'. Broadly, extension strategies can be split into five categories:

1. The development of new markets for existing products by isolating areas where the product is not used and modifying it to suit those particular requirements. Battery shavers were introduced to fulfil the need for electric shavers when users were away from electricity supplies. There has been considerable effort to expand the usage of computers and models have been developed to meet the needs and budgets of small firms.

2. The development of new uses for existing products such as the application of red l.c.d. (liquid crystal displays, used for example in calculators and watches). Nylon is another example of a product which has gone through many extensions. Originally introduced for military purposes in the manufacture of parachutes and rope, it developed as a fabric, making good use of the expansion in the women's stocking and clothing market, and more recently being incorporated in tyre manufacture.

3. The development of more frequent use of a product. This can be achieved either by altering its image, as in the case of turkeys which have changed from being a Christmas treat into an all-year round food, or by emphasising special characteristics such as convenience and quality in the frozen foods market.

4. The development of a wider range of products. There has been an explosion in the flavours of ice cream available, putting the manufacturer who can supply many different varieties at a significant advantage. Also the class of ice creams has expanded from inexpensive every-day brands to exclusive and costly types with unusual and exotic combinations of flavours.

5. The development of styling changes which demonstrate the newness of the most recent product. Car manufacturers are an obvious example. They create new designs which leave old models looking outdated. Often Mark II variations include technical improvements as well, and such changes enable manufacturers to modify their pricing policy to suit new market conditions.

Awareness of a product's life cycle enables firms to plan their extension strategies well in advance so that they continue to control the product's development rather than finding themselves reacting to unanticipated market developments. However, there are dangers associated with extension strategies. The replacement of an existing model must not leave distributors with large stocks which they cannot get rid of, and too much variety can cause problems for consumers. In the late 1960s, a rapid expansion in the types of

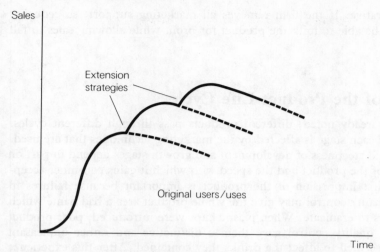

Fig. 5.4: Extension strategies to the product life cycle

paint finish caused problems in the market. Uncertainty, coupled with insufficient knowledge of the different properties of each type, sometimes led to confusion and resulted in the consumer not buying any kind of paint.

The length of the maturity stage depends on the nature of the product and the marketing strategies employed. A much improved substitute can kill off a product by removing the need for it. Calculators have effectively removed the market for slide-rules, electric light bulbs replaced the demand for paraffin lamps, the motor car reduced the demand for train travel, and so on. Some products such as fashion goods have very short maturity stages because it is in the nature of the business to replace styles frequently; while some medicines, such as aspirins, have had a long and stable maturity stage.

5.5.5 Decline
Eventually, all products fall into the decline stage when the market for the product has been superseded by a technological or styling change which replaces the demand. For example, the development of tough, water-based paint has made significant inroads into the traditional market for oil-based paint. Alternatively, interest in the product may fade, leading to a rapid reduction in sales. When this happens, the level of competition for the declining market may increase and those manufacturers still involved have to enlarge their market share to maintain output at sufficiently profitable levels. Expenditure in support of the product falls and prices become keener in an effort to liquidate stocks rapidly. The number of distribution outlets is progressively cut back. Over-capacity is a major problem and fewer firms can remain in the market. The collapse of many skateboard manufacturers is attributable to intense competition in a market which is no longer growing, as is the drastic reduction in firms making calculators. Alternatively, the decline stage may be

the most lucrative. If the firm removes all marketing support, so reducing costs, it may be able to milk the product for profit while allowing sales to fall slowly.

5.6 Use of the Product Life Cycle

As we have already noted, different products pass through different cycles. The length of each stage is affected by the marketing techniques that are used. The length and steepness of development and growth stages depend in part on the newness of the product and the speed with which it gains consumer acceptance. The first impression of the product is important because failures in design and quality control may give the whole product area a bad name which can take years to eradicate. When plastic cups were introduced, poor product research and quality control gave them a distinctive and rather unpleasant smell which seemed to affect the drinks they contained. After this experience it took many years to overcome consumer resistance to any form of plastic cup.

Newness and complexity both require considerable time and money for the market to be 'educated' and the need explained. Small firms are often at a disadvantage because they do not have the resources to stand this early strain, or the working capital to provide sufficient after-sales service. Often, the development stage takes longer when many people are involved in the decision to use a new product, especially if it is replacing an existing product. Suppose a range of bearings for the motor industry was developed using new materials and manufacturing techniques. The firm that came up with the product would have to persuade the motor industry of the advantages, and take on producers of the current type whose supposed expertise will carry weight in the decision over whether to change. For existing producers a change will make their production lines obsolete and they will lose a major market. If the new bearing is accepted, once it has become established it is likely to have a long life cycle.

Pricing is important in determining the shape of the cycle. From the outset, the manufacturer must decide whether to choose a high price and 'skim' the market, with the risk of attracting too much competition, or to price cheaply and aim for greater and more rapid market penetration. The decision is partly dependent on the expected life of the product but a low price from the start may cause sales to grow quickly and fade equally fast. Because of the relatively low profits resulting from this policy, firms may not have sufficient resources to develop extension strategies or research new products. In addition, it is easier to reduce rather than raise prices as time goes on. At the same time, the pricing decision cannot be taken without considering the image of the firm and its product. People expecting a high-price, 'snob' product from a company may be suspicious of an inexpensive addition to the range, and conversely a manufacturer with a 'down-market' image may find a serious credibility gap if he tries to break into the quality market.

It would be wrong for all firms to set their marketing strategy to follow a product life cycle in a rigid way. However, as a tool in product planning it has valuable applications through its indication of probable movements, but it is often difficult to determine exactly where a product is on the cycle. Variations in sales from year to year will occur and it is important not to misinterpret these as indications that a product is declining, when in fact a combination of factors is creating minor fluctuations. This is more easily said than done. Certainty only comes with hindsight and by the time it is clear that decline has set in, sales may have fallen disastrously. The firm may find itself in a market with no easy way of leaving it.

If a marketing director has determined that a product is reaching the end of its useful life then it is difficult to save it, since there will be competing demands on resources from other products. Removal of all the sales and promotion props from a product so that they may be used to develop a new idea guarantees decline. However, careful manipulation of the pricing or promotion factors might have moved the product into a consolidated maturity stage.

Sometimes it can be advantageous not to follow the product life cycle as in the case of Oxo. By 1956 sales of Oxo cubes had been falling for eight years. The product had been around for a long time and sales were strongest during the Second World War when meat had not been easily available. Post-war affluence suggested that the market had shifted and the product was in decline. It would have been reasonable to drop it. However, the company decided to relaunch the product. It repackaged the cubes and sold them in a new size. The sales force was expanded and more was spent on advertising. Within five years sales had risen by 35 per cent. This example underlines the importance of experience and intuition in marketing, and the need to take risks when a particular theory suggests one course of action. The product life cycle alone cannot provide all the answers.

Thus the firm has to set a balance between following the cycle in a pre-determined way and ignoring it completely. Both extreme courses can cause unnecessary expense, and fail to milk the greatest profits from a product. The success of the balance depends largely on the extent of information reaching the firm both about its own products and those of its competitors. Judgement and risk taking are prime requirements for a good marketing director.

5.7 The Market Plan

The objectives of the firm will usually include a profit requirement. This can provide the basis for new product development and modifications to existing products. Initially the firm should examine each of its products to see where they are on the product life cycle. This will give an indication of likely future performance and the marketing strategy needed to support them. Sales revenue can be compared with the expenditure involved in achieving the volume of sales. At the same time careful examination of the market to take account of competitors' actions and possible extension strategies will help to keep the firm ahead of the field. It is the job of the marketing department to decide when a product should be phased out, and to develop replacements. An estimate of the new products required in the medium term gives an indication of how much research is required, allowing for failures. Thus the firm may decide that it can grow by launching six major products in a five-year span, four of them within the first three years. It has to decide which products and brands are the major priorities for use of limited resources.

Sales volume is important because sales must be sufficient to cover overheads as well as direct costs of manufacture. Break-even analysis can be used to estimate the minimum acceptable sales level. Inevitably, there is a measure of risk involved in any new launch but an attempt to quantify it through probability and decision trees enables a figure to be put on likely returns. Included in any new product development should be an estimate of how soon the development costs will be recouped. If the pay-back period is too long there is a danger that the product will have been replaced before development costs have been recovered. The firm has to estimate future revenue and costs to calculate a profit figure and those future cash items must be calculated at present day values. Inflows of cash are worth more the earlier they arrive because they can be used for new projects. **Discounted cash flow** is a method of taking this opportunity cost of projects into consideration.

Setting profit targets will depend on the nature of the markets. A mass market with established strong brands will require heavy advertising and promotion for a new entrant to gain any market share. This means that the sales volume will have to be high to sustain promotional support at a competitive level. Where the firm holds a large market share, new products should yield profits well above the minimum required. The same applies when the firm is using its distinctive competence and is at an advantage over its competitors.

As the plan is built up and communicated to the relevant departments in the firm, it begins to fill with detail. Decisions are taken on how the products will be launched or re-launched; this involves the type of advertising, packaging, distribution and pricing. Gradually a full picture of the firm's intentions will emerge. The timing of the launch or change in marketing strategy is set. Decisions on test markets and the way the firm will handle the findings all go into the blue-print for action. Planning does not guarantee success but it provides a thought-out approach to achieving the firm's objectives and a yardstick against which performance can be judged.

Work Section

A. Revision Questions

A1 What is product evaluation?

A2 What are the disadvantages of defining a market in a narrow way?

A3 What are the advantages and disadvantages of diversification of the product line?

A4 What type of companies are the principal product innovators, and why?

A5 What is meant by 'distinctive competence'?

A6 What are the two objectives of the patent system?

A7 What are the four main stages of the product life cycle?

A8 What is meant by 'skimming the market' and 'market penetration'?

A9 How might the marketing strategy for a product vary through its life cycle?

A10 List the five categories of extension strategies.

A11 What are the difficulties of using the product life cycle?

A12 How can a firm decide on the number of new products it should develop?

B. Exercises/Case Studies

B1 Alfred Dunhill Limited was founded in 1907 as a tobacco specialist. Based in London, the company rapidly became internationally famous for its pipes and other smokers' accessories. From 1924, the company opened shops in other countries to achieve wider distribution through its own outlets and other distributors in all major markets throughout the world.

The end of 1974 was a watershed for Dunhill. Immediately prior to that time, the company had experienced unprecedented growth, both in turnover and profits (see table), but this growth was based almost entirely on the demand for the Dunhill Rollagas lighter. A new management team had been appointed on the retirement of two senior directors, and it took over at the time of the initial repercussions of the oil crisis, which threatened to plunge the world into a major recession in consumer spending.

By this time the name of Dunhill was synonymous with luxury smoking merchandise, but smoking was starting to come under increasing attack for health reasons. It was felt that the long-term effect of this could be damaging, both to the tobacco-related business (including lighters) and ultimately to the prestige of Dunhill itself.

The company had great financial strength, but was dangerously dependent on the sale of the Rollagas lighter, of which the greatest proportion was purchased by the Japanese. The result for the financial year 1974/75 showed that lighters had contributed approximately 50 per cent of total turnover and over 60 per cent of profit.

As a result the company embarked on a comprehensive evaluation of the strengths and weaknesses of the business with the objective of identifying a clearly defined development strategy for the future.

Financial record (£m.)

	1970/71	1971/72	1972/73	1973/74	1974/75
Turnover:	9.0	10.4	13.3	17.0	19.8
Profit before tax:	1.8	2.7	4.4	5.9	6.2

a. List (a) the strengths; (b) the weaknesses of the Dunhill business in 1975.
b. What long-term objectives should have been established?
c. Given the strengths and weaknesses, how could the business develop in the future?
   (With acknowledgements to Tony Greener, Managing Director, Dunhill Ltd.)

B2 In 1962 Anita manufactured the first desk top electronic calculator. Unlike today's models, it was large and performed only a few functions. It was also expensive. Manufacture of the calculator was labour intensive and the idea was copied by the Japanese who were able to gain a price advantage since labour was relatively cheap in Japan. As a result they dominated the small market until 1972.

Meanwhile, in America, one of the 'spin-offs' of the Apollo space programme was the development of the silicon chip. This enabled the circuits which had been soldered on to circuit boards to be shrunk on to a chip of silicon. Texas Instruments manufactured the first single chip and Bowmar, a Canadian company, used this to introduce a hand-held calculator. Sinclair, a British company, was the first to realise the potential of the calculator for the consumer market.

The first successes in the consumer market led to a mushroom growth from the Japanese companies previously making desk top models. By this stage the market possibilities were beginning to become apparent and both Texas and Rockwell, two massive semi-conductor companies, entered the market. Sales took off as a result of the competition and low prices, following mass production which reduced unit over-heads. Sales grew by 20 per cent in 1976, although the beginnings of the maturity stage were indicated by the appearance of seasonal sales. Prices had fallen dramatically – the Sinclair Executive started at £79 for a four function $(+, -, \times, \div)$ machine. By 1977 it was possible to buy a four function calculator for around £5. Part of the reason why prices fell was the rapid rate of technological advance. Originally, the chips were a problem because only around 2 per cent of the production was of sufficient quality. As chip manufacture improved, the cost of the chip fell. Most of the remaining costs came from labour since the manufacture of calculators involved assembling over 250 parts. Again, technological improvements reduced the number of parts, in some cases to as few as four basic pieces.

Initially calculators were sold solely as office equipment, but as the consumer market grew, outlets such as Boots, Dixons, Laskys and Currys came to be used. This, coupled with volume sales and rapid changes in technology, has speeded up the life cycle and led to particular selling problems as new models quickly supersede old ones. The product life lasts about eight months for the basic model and up to two years for the programmables. Manufacturers have been under pressure to keep up with the market's demand for new products and technological innovation. There have been some disasters. For example, Bowmar, which started the ball rolling, developed its own chip-making capacity, but the costs involved nearly bankrupted the company. In 1970 Commodore bought up the Bowmar calculator business. Other victims include many small firms which collapsed under the concerted pressure of the giant companies. Rockwell bought Anita in 1973 and closed it in 1976, and the parent company has shifted its emphasis to business machines.

Against this background of the price-cutting war, Sinclair emerged strongly. The company was too small to withstand losses similar to those sustained by some of the large companies, but shrewd analysis of the situation and advanced design kept it profitable. Unlike most other companies, Sinclair did not build up its own chip making capacity, although the chips it used were designed by the company. This policy gave it greater flexibility and freedom to change designs, as well as avoiding the need to invest huge amounts of money in the production of chips.

The market is changing all the time. Developments in the products and the use of calculator technology in other areas such as the displays in digital watches have kept the industry expanding. In the late 1970s, the opening-up of the school and university markets meant that sales could remain high.

Meanwhile the competitive pressure has continued to take its toll of companies. Sinclair, for example, ran into problems, and in 1979 its calculator interests were bought by Binatone.

(Adapted from 'Carving up the Calculators', by Simon Caulkin in *Management Today*, March 1977)

Questions:

a. Explain the structure of the industry.
b. Trace the stages of the product life cycle that the calculator has gone through explaining your reasoning.
c. How has the marketing strategy changed since 1962?
d. What do you consider the key factors of the mix to have been?

C. Essay Questions

C1 How can the product life cycle be used to help build up an overall marketing strategy for a product?

C2 'The product life cycle is a piece of theory that has no practical application
in real-life marketing.' Discuss.

C3 Assess the short-run and long-run impact on the marketing strategies of a
British car manufacturing firm of a further increase in the UK price of
petrol. (Cambridge Local Examinations Syndicate 1976.2.7)

C4 Explain the expression 'product life cycle'. How should management pay
attention to this concept? (Cambridge Local Examinations Syndicate
1977.2.7)

C5 Could the patent system be said to be operating in restraint of trade?

C6 How might a company plan its product policy over the next five years?

Chapter 6

Distribution

Objective: *To show the importance of distribution in the marketing process and to explain the different channels of distribution, suggesting factors that affect the choice.*

Synopsis: *Distribution covers every stage between the factory and the final destination of the product. There are various possible channels of distribution, either direct or involving middlemen. The choice of channel is dependent on the control required by the manufacturer, the type of market and product, the nature of the company and the type of middleman.*

Plan of the chapter

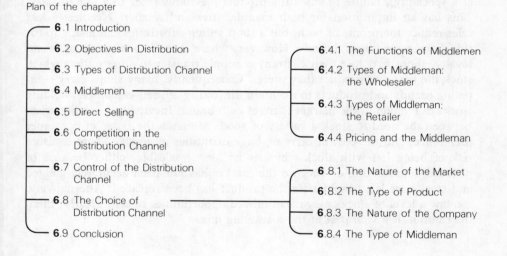

6.1 Introduction

Most products are purchased in relatively small quantities compared to their volume of manufacture, and the industrial or household basket of goods is made up of a wide variety of products from different firms. Bringing the product to its final consumer is the job of distribution. The distribution method chosen must reflect the image and the nature of the product itself. A firm making jam intended for a wide market would not choose to sell it solely through Fortnum and Mason, while an expensive and exclusive perfume would probably not be distributed through a supermarket. How to distribute products is not an easy decision, and failure to choose the best type of distribution will damage the product's sales.

With mass-production, output has become centralised into a few factories, producing large quantities of standardised goods. By concentrating output in this way, major economies of scale have been achieved, but while the trend to mass production has continued it has brought with it problems of distribution. The market requires the complete opposite – namely, small quantities, variety and irregular purchases dispersed over a wide geographical area. It is important that the increased costs of distribution are not greater than the cost advantages of mass production, and that the economies of scale are not lost because the distribution network is not suited to the product and the market. Since sales are dependent on the availability of products, a manufacturer with high fixed costs of production needs to be sure that he is reaching the market he wants, in sufficient quantities.

Convenience goods are low unit value goods which, by definition, are purchased frequently, have close substitutes and must be easily available on the market. Since brand loyalty is low (otherwise the product would become more of a speciality), failure to stock the product inevitably leads to a loss of sales. This has an implication for both manufacturer and retailer. Needlessly lost sales reduce the profits of both, but a shop selling substitutes can make up for this from competitors' brands. However, where there is a measure of brand loyalty, shops may lose their custom, as people transfer to other outlets which stock the brand or product they prefer. Consequently, many shops carry competing brands and products to maintain the loyalty of their customers, holding stocks in relation to the market share of each brand. Inevitably a conflict arises between the need to stock a variety of goods to match the range of consumer preference, and the cost of carrying large quantities of goods. There is also a risk of being left with stock which is no longer saleable, either because of physical deterioration or because the market has not been accurately gauged and stocks are left unsold after the product has been replaced. Alternatively, too low a level of stocks may mean missed opportunities to sell. Clearly, then, distribution is a vital part of the marketing mix.

6.2 Objectives in Distribution

The broad aim of distribution is simple. All firms set out to make their products available at the right place at the right time. Distribution is part of the whole operation of a business, and the method chosen depends on the objectives set for cost (and hence profit), control over the product, sales volume and market coverage.

The method of distribution must be the best consistent with cost and the other needs of the company. It must increase the total profitability of the organisation. Not all methods allow the manufacturer the same control over the product once it leaves his premises, and this influences the distribution decision. For a high-value, fragile product some manufacturer control over distribution may be desirable and necessary. It is less important for simple, inexpensive goods.

Objectives in other areas affect the distribution channel chosen. The existing and projected market share and the degree of market coverage are important for they provide a general indication of the type of outlet required. The expected density of the market will partially determine whether distribution should be carried out by the firm or handed over to a specialist. Some firms set strategic objectives which concentrate on production and product research, in which case distribution is organised by an outside firm. Constraints such as level of expertise in marketing, and limited financial resources also suggest that external assistance is required for distribution. A new company may have little knowledge of retail outlets and it may be best to allow a wholesaler to deal with the product once it has been manufactured.

6.3 Types of Distribution Channel

The distribution channel covers the stages through which the manufactured goods pass from producer to consumer. The channel refers to the route taken by the ownership of the product – or 'title' – not to the physical movement of the goods. Thus a commodity dealer engaged in the buying and selling of copper may own hundreds of tons of copper without actually taking possession of it, or even seeing it. A new channel of distribution starts if the product is substantially altered. Swedish timber destined to be made into furniture in the

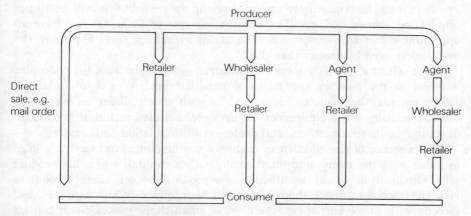

Fig. 6.1: Types of distribution channel

south of England goes through one channel of distribution. Once the furniture is made, it starts a new channel up to the final owner.

Ideally, the channel of distribution should be viewed as a total system but there is often competition between those involved. There are many alternatives, and a manufacturer may use several different channels for the same product range. Competition may be desirable, enhancing price and quality, although it does not always lead to the most efficient system.

A typical channel for consumer goods may look something like this:

Producer ───▶Wholesaler ───▶Retailer ───▶Consumer.

But there are many variations. The range is shown in Fig. 6.1.
Theoretically the agent, who does not take title to the goods, should not be included in the distribution channel, but where used, his role is so important in getting the product to the consumer that he merits a place.

6.4 Middlemen

Except in a few cases it was not practical for a manufacturer to deal directly with the final consumer because of the disparity in quantity and variety of the goods produced, and the needs of the market. To overcome this the major categories of middlemen, retailers and wholesalers, were established. Recently, however, there has been a trend to bypass as many stages as possible in order to cut costs. The functions of the middlemen still have to be carried out, and bypassing the stages does not always lead to more efficient distribution. It is only practicable when dealing with large customers who buy in bulk.

The manufacturer who carries out his own distribution has to finance the cost of it. The opportunity cost of the resources tied up in stocks, personnel, administration and handling can be measured in terms of the return the manufacturer expects on his business. If the firm expects a 10 per cent return on its assets then the opportunity cost of carrying the distribution will be 10 per cent of the money tied up. The distribution cost of £100,000 will have an opportunity cost of £10,000 p.a. The savings resulting from bypassing the middlemen must be greater than this.

Direct selling is more frequent for industrial products because the order size is large, or the product specific to a particular job. A piece of industrial equipment may be made to order, and in such a case direct selling makes sense, especially if the equipment requires sophisticated technical knowledge in setting up its specifications, and dealing with installation and service.

The existence of the middleman enables a manufacturer, indirectly, to keep in touch with the many, and often small, outlets through which his product sells. Obviously it would be difficult for a producer of convenience goods to visit and service all those shops which sell his product. While he might deal directly with major customers, the mass of small shops makes direct contact with each uneconomic. However, the wholesaler can sell a considerable total quantity of merchandise to each store, comprising a variety of different products, each in relatively small quantities.

By using a middleman firms can make use of his specialist skills and knowledge of the distribution system (see Fig. 6.2). Consider a situation where three manufacturers sell products in five outlets. If each manufacturer directly approaches each outlet then fifteen transactions will occur. Using a wholesaler, this is cut to eight – three between manufacturer and wholesaler and five between wholesaler and retail outlets. However, it does mean a loss of control of the operation by the manufacturer and a greater need to rely on the ability of the wholesaler.

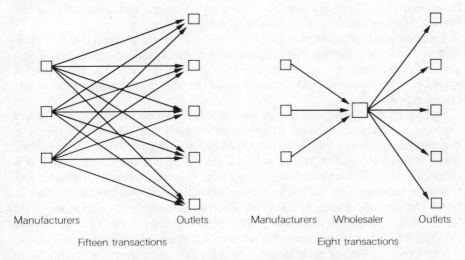

| Manufacturers | Outlets | Manufacturers | Wholesaler | Outlets |

| Fifteen transactions | | Eight transactions | | |

Fig. 6.2: The transactions involved in a distribution system

6.4.1 The Functions of Middlemen
Middlemen fulfil two key functions in the distribution process:

1. Agent and bulk breaker.
2. Stockholder.

1. A wholesaler acts as a buying agent for the retailer, laying in stock that the retailer wants, and as a selling agent for the producer, providing merchandise for the retailer's consideration. It is the job of the wholesaler to break down his stock to manageable amounts, and anticipate the needs of the retailer. At the same time the wholesaler may promote certain brands in the trade, and also promote his business, so persuading more retailers to buy through him. In this way, trade promotion may lead to an increase in sales.
2. The stockholding function and its associated risks represent the most important service to the manufacturer. Stockholding provides a buffer between the variety and irregularity of purchases and the long, standardised runs of production. It also adds value to the stocks. Goods that are required

in the West Country but manufactured in Scotland have no value unless they can be brought to the market; similarly, if there is a six-month delay in delivery, those goods fall in value. Provided a local wholesaler has stocks of the relevant product the sale can be made.

If there are many stages in the distribution channel, the stock requirements will be greater, but there will be less danger of shortages. However, stockholding is costly in terms of the buildings, insurance and administration, transport and handling equipment. Money tied up in stocks has an opportunity cost – that is, the cost of lost returns from the alternative use to which that money could have been put. There are also risks involved, through technological obsolescence, deterioration of quality, theft and fire.

Technological obsolescence is the result of product development. The advent of colour television has reduced sales of black and white models. Transistors largely replaced valves in the hi-fi market, so reducing the value of stocks of valve amplifiers. At a time of rapid changes in technology this danger has increased.

Styling changes also lead to the loss in value of older merchandise. In the clothing industry the arrival of the new season's fashions means that the demand for last year's look is removed. In order to overcome the worst of this, many stores have end-of-season sales to get rid of old stock, albeit at much reduced prices. Similar problems occur in the motor, household appliance and furniture industries. A shift in consumer priorities can have the same effect as tastes change, and products fall from interest. If households decide to spend less of their income on electrical goods then the value of stocks of these will decline, whilst the longer period it takes to sell them will increase their costs.

The problem for the middleman is that he has taken over the stockholding function but is not party to company decisions surrounding its product developments. Nevertheless companies need to retain the goodwill of their distributors in order to ensure that their products will continue to be stocked.

One way round obsolescence is to inform wholesalers and retailers of impending change so that they can run down their stocks of old products before the new one is launched. However, it is difficult to maintain secrecy. Once the information escapes that a new model is about to be introduced, surprise is lost and competitors are warned in advance of changes that could be of use to them. Few wholesalers or retailers carry only one company's products so there is limited loyalty to any manufacturer, and keeping the innovation quiet is virtually impossible. One way of maintaining the goodwill of the distribution chain is to compensate for unsold stock when a replacement product is put on the market with no advance warning.

6.4.2 Types of Middleman: The Wholesaler
Wholesaling falls into two categories: those who do not take title to the goods, such as agents and brokers, and wholesalers who actually purchase the goods and pass them on.

Agents and brokers exist to bring buyers and sellers together by acting as intermediaries. The manufacturer may use his own agents which has the advantage of guaranteeing loyalty to the firm and increasing motivation. However, the manufacturer's agent may not have the breadth of contacts of an independent agent. Since the independent agent is likely to deal in several, not necessarily competing, lines, he will come across a wider range of clients and may be able to develop a hitherto unused outlet for the product. However, although paid on a commission basis like the manufacturer's agent, his livelihood does not depend on the fortunes of one company, and he is less likely to undertake 'missionary selling' for any one manufacturer; nor does he have the specialised knowledge and information of the product that comes from a full-time job selling for one firm. A firm has to decide whether to use its own agents and rely on their more concentrated skills, or employ an outside agent on the grounds of greater knowledge of clients. In part, this decision depends on the product and the market. If the product is of relatively low unit value and the market is dispersed, then the firm is more likely to hand it over to an independent agent.

Wholesalers fulfil a different function, in that ownership of the product brings with it a wider range of services and risks. Although there has been growth in wholesalers selling direct to the public, by far their largest market is the retail sector.

6.4.3 Types of Middleman: The Retailer
A retailer is an outlet involved in the sale of goods to their ultimate purchaser for personal use. In practice many retailers provide goods for business, as well as personal use. A hardware shop may sell goods to home-owners for do-it-yourself use, but it may also sell part of its merchandise to contractors involved in local building. The retail sector has considerable economic significance because it is a major source of employment and the place where most personal income is spent.

Opening a shop is relatively easy, but retailing is highly competitive and there are many failures. Look at your local high street over a period of time and you will see shops closing down or opening largely in response to competition and expected market activity. The prime job of a retailer is to service his customers' needs. Looking after the interests of any particular manufacturer is of secondary importance and this can be frustrating for the producer who wants to push his products at the point-of-sale. That is not to say that the retailer's fortunes are completely independent of his suppliers but rather to emphasise the difference in interests and objectives. For instance, when a product is in considerable demand, the store will make a greater effort to stock and present it well.

The retail sector ranges from the small corner shop with a limited product range, to out-of-town hypermarkets such as 'Asda' which provide for most consumer requirements in one complex. Many shops are sole-traders, owned by the man who runs them; others, such as MacFisheries, are owned by manufacturers (Unilever) which will stock their own products, although not exclusively; others are chain stores such as Marks and Spencer which stock only their own branded (St Michael) goods, made under licence by manufacturers.

In recent years there has been a shift to larger retail units that can offer a wide range of merchandise at highly competitive prices achieved through cheaper operating costs. Although the public image of the corner shop is better than that of many large stores, the bulk of the nation's purchasing power goes into the supermarkets and department stores. The large store has the advantage of discounts on bulk purchases and division of labour, with specialists in each major area of operation. Set against this is the charge that they lack the personal approach and they cannot provide the highly individual attention of a small local shop. Some of the large London stores have overcome this to a degree, but fast-flow supermarkets, where the only contact is at the checkout till, do not aim to offer personal service. Instead the product needs to sell itself, and efficient use of personnel is reflected in competitive prices. Many of the larger stores stock 'own-brand' products along with the established names and they can make far more use of local and national advertising. A chain with branches spread through the country has the advantage of frequent and repeated exposure of its name and with this comes some implied or explicit guarantee of consistent quality. Unlike smaller stores, the large operations have significant overheads which have to be met through high volume sales.

6.4.4 Pricing and the Middleman

The middleman makes his profit by charging a mark-up for his services. It usually follows that a distribution chain using several stages makes the product more expensive to the final consumer, although expertise and economies of scale in middleman functions may avoid this. However, the flexibility of price changes is reduced. Consider the following example:

Example: A firm manufacturing novelty products for the tourist trade distributes through wholesalers and retailers. The wholesaler mark-up is 50 per cent and the retailer mark-up is 100 per cent. The ex-factory price of a model lighthouse is £3. By the time it is sold to the retailer the price has risen to £4.50 (£3 + 50%). The price to the final consumer is £9 (£4.50 + 100%). The firm receives only one third of the final price. If his costs rise by £1 it will add £3 to the final price.

A larger firm with its own delivery fleet cuts out the wholesaler and sells direct to the retailer, giving him a mark-up of 120 per cent as an incentive to stock the product. Costs to the firm include its distribution and storage expenses, and the ex-factory price of its lighthouse is £3.50. It sells to the final consumer at £7.70 (£3.50 + 120%). An increase in costs of £1 will only raise the final price by £2.20, and the competitive price advantage increases as well as enabling the firm to give the retailer a greater return.

6.5 Direct Selling

Direct selling by the manufacturer to the retailer may be appropriate in certain situations. Direct selling forces the manufacturer to carry larger stocks and finance the extra costs, but it does enable distribution to be highly co-ordinated because there are no intermediaries with different and possibly conflicting objectives.

Where the market is geographically concentrated, and served by large retail stores, or where there is a central buying office for a chain of shops, the approach is most likely to be direct from the manufacturer since the size of orders justifies the effort put into the sale. From the retailer's position, discounts on bulk buying make a short chain desirable because the retailer can pass the discounts on and offer goods at lower prices, encouraging higher demand.

If the product is fragile or perishable firms may want to control it as far as possible to ensure its quality is maintained. The longer the distribution chain, the more likely damage will occur, and where the product will deteriorate with time the fastest, and hence shortest, channel of distribution must be used. This usually involves direct selling to the retailer or, in some cases, direct to the customer through mail order or door-to-door selling.

For industrial products, a combination of channels is frequently employed. While the bulk of the output may be sold direct to its final user, spare parts or odd-ends of production runs may be sold through a wholesaler. For example, a manufacturer of parts for the motor industry may sell most of his output direct to the car maker, but a spare part scheme is likely to be run through appointed dealers. The steel industry manufactures to certain specifications and distributes direct to its customers. However, the order size may be different from the optimum production run output, and the balance may be held in stock or sold to a wholesaler awaiting a small order.

6.6 Competition in the Distribution Channel

Distribution channels change, especially when new developments in retailing occur such as the rise of the supermarket, and now, the hypermarket. Competition occurs both at the same level within the distribution chain, and also between different levels. At the same level retailers or wholesalers may expand the product lines they deal with. The introduction of clothing at Tesco or food at Marks and Spencer provided new competition for the traditional outlets. Changes are usually the result of consumers' preference for doing the bulk of their shopping in one store, or because the retailer chooses new products which provide a higher mark-up than existing merchandise. The store wants to maximise its sales and react to changes which increase the customer flow or the profit on each purchase. Manufacturers may want to increase their sales and market coverage and expand into new outlets because they see opportunities there. Greater sales may lead to further cuts in the cost of production.

Competition between the stages of distribution occurs as manufacturers or intermediaries see opportunities to cut the cost of distribution. Thus a manufacturer may decide to shoulder more of the wholesaling function by using his own agents to operate in areas which have previously been serviced by wholesalers. Retailers may sell to institutions, so taking some of the market away from wholesalers, or the producer may try to sell direct to the consumer or through its own retail stores.

6.7 Control of the Distribution Channel

Competition is created not only by cost considerations and service provided, but also by the degree to which the distribution network is controlled by each of the stages. When a manufacturer passes his product on to the middleman, he no longer controls its destiny. If the product is in great demand, and the dealers receive good mark-ups, then it will be an attractive product to distribute. In this situation the manufacturer will have a greater say on how its distribution should be handled by the intermediaries. Alternatively, the prestige of a particular retailer may be greater than the product. It then becomes important for the manufacturer to persuade the retailer to stock it. In this way the image of the store may rub off on to the product. Harrods, for example, is much better known than many of the products it sells. Locally the corner shop may carry prestige and a guarantee of quality.

The growth of larger stores and self-service outlets has transferred control from manufacturers towards retailers. The existence of large retail chains, and bulk purchases, combined with greater emphasis on store layout and sales maximisation, make them important power blocs. This has restricted the freedom of the manufacturer to organise the distribution of his product. The size of the retail stores has expanded because of greater customer mobility enlarging the size of the market, and cost pressures which have forced them to use labour and space more efficiently.

The wholesaler's position is less clear. A wholesaler with access to a wide market will be in greater demand than one operating in a very limited sphere, and therefore is better able to dictate terms. However, wholesalers have been under pressure because retailers are increasingly buying in bulk direct from manufacturers. Wholesalers may be left with small shops to service where there are fewer economies of scale.

6.8 The Choice of Distribution Channel

Several factors are important in selecting the distribution channel for a product. Inevitably, since every product and every market has characteristics which distinguish it from others, there is no hard and fast rule which determines how best it will be distributed. Every product must be judged on its specific requirements. However, some general ideas can be laid down. There are four areas which need consideration:

1. The nature of the market.
2. The type of product.
3. The nature of the company.
4. The type of middleman.

We will look at each of these in turn.

6.8.1 The Nature of the Market

From market research, the firm will have discovered the size of the market – either present or potential – and whether it is likely to expand or contract. In addition, information on the distribution of customers, their age groups and buying habits affects the choice of outlets. A widely dispersed market calls for a different distribution approach from a closely packed one, and not all regions behave in the same way towards a product, or purchase it in the same shops. Some areas have highly seasonal populations with the tourist trade swelling the demand for products in the summer. This could lead to a greater need for wholesalers with stockholding facilities to service those areas. Thus regional differences become important in setting up a distribution network, and may lead to several different channels being used in order to cover the range of requirements.

The distribution pattern will be heavily influenced by the existing consumer buying patterns. If people tend to make most purchases of German sausage in specialist delicatessen shops rather than supermarkets, then an importer would choose to distribute through specialist outlets. There has been considerable growth recently in the 'cash and carry' outlets where purchases are made in bulk (by household standards). The enormous growth in freezer ownership created a change in buying patterns. To meet this demand specialist frozen food shops like Bejams have grown up. But while there is considerable change going on in the retail market – for example, the mushroom growth of discount hi-fi shops – the consumer is often remarkably slow to adapt to it. Once accustomed to buying vegetables at the market or greengrocer, a householder may refuse to buy supermarket products; the same is true for meats where an equation between packaging and tastelessness has grown up in the minds of many consumers.

6.8.2 The Type of Product

The problems of distributing Devon clotted cream, or soap powder, or a complete computer system are very different. Perishable goods need as direct a channel as possible. A direct channel has the advantage of reducing the time and handling of the product. It also enables the manufacturer to exercise greater control over the product after it leaves the factory and it increases the contact between producer and consumer. Where quality is an important selling point the manufacturer may extend 'franchises' to a limited number of retailers. These retailers are the sole suppliers of the product and the local market must buy through them. Thus there is an incentive to maintain standards.

D

Technically complex goods lend themselves to more direct channels of distribution so that handling can be reduced; but more important, so that the link between producer and consumer is fairly close. For such products there is little point in duplicating the technical skills at each level, so direct channels are more likely to be used. Some firms manufacturing industrial goods operate directly with the customer. Xerox deals with the installation and maintenance of its copying machines; IBM works directly with the customer in setting the specifications of computer requirements and follows through with installation and maintenance, and so on.

Convenience goods present different requirements since they need wide coverage for large sales levels to be achieved. The retailer's role is very important to the manufacturer because if one brand is not on the shelves sales will be lost to a competitor. The similarity of the products means that substitutes are frequently made. Any form of brand identity and loyalty is largely created by advertising and promotion. In the supermarket the selling side is relegated to that of display. When substitutes are bought, the store is not told of any particular brand preference so that the flow of information back from the customer is restricted. However, at least there is likely to be more information if there are fewer stages between producer and consumer.

The intensive distribution necessary for convenience goods can involve higher costs because it has to include low volume outlets as well as supermarkets and large department stores.

For products where there is considerable brand loyalty, distribution can be more selective. Concentrating the selling effort to a few outlets may bring a better sales performance because the sales work is more thorough. A shift from widespread to selective distribution returns more control to the manufacturer. If the demand is strong retailers will want to handle the product because they are likely to gain sales and this enables the manufacturer to be more discriminating in the choice of store that distributes it.

New products present particular problems. If they are unlike anything already on the market there are no immediate guides to their distribution either from past experience or from competitors' methods. Fear within the trade of a new product whose sales they feel will be uncertain can have two opposing effects. Either wholesalers will be reluctant to take them on, and so direct approaches to retailers will have to be made, or, because retailers are wary, the burden of distribution will be given to wholesalers who can use their specialist knowledge of the market to choose the best approach. In either case, considerable promotion will be required both within the trade and directed at the final consumer to convince middlemen that a market for the product does exist, and sizeable mark-ups will be allowed as an incentive to the trade to handle the product. In extreme circumstances unfavourable trade reaction may cause a product to be scrapped. Figure 6.3 shows the main reasons grocery buyers refuse to stock new products.

Products such as Christmas puddings or sunglasses and suntan lotion, which face a seasonal demand, create the need for a stockholding function. Either the manufacturer will undertake this or he will be forced into using wholesalers.

Reasons for refusal *to stock new products*	*Per cent of buyers asked, giving the reason* *1970*	*1980*
No product advantage	56	71
No shelf space	39	42
Poor product quality	66	42
Little advertising support	57	45
Declining market	51	52
No introductory terms	25	21
Product from a small company	7	3

Fig. 6.3: Reasons for refusal to stock products

(*Source*: KAE New Products in Grocers (1980))

The alternative is to provide a product range which allows for batch production times to suit the seasons, replacing goods out of season with those that are in. However, this is not always easy and can often be very disruptive of production schedules.

6.8.3 The Nature of the Company

Large firms with strong markets for their products tend to deal with their own distribution as far as possible. They have the financial resources to undertake the wholesalers' stockholding functions and there is often a greater desire to control the product further along the line. If the operation is large enough to develop specialists in distribution within the firm, their greater motivation to sell the product may increase sales. There are considerable economies of scale to be gained in stockholding and administration. Promotion can be more closely co-ordinated. This is especially true for firms which have their own retail outlets where in-store promotion can match the rest of the mix. However, it leaves the company to take on all the risks and can create serious cash flow problems. Naturally, complete control of the distribution system in this way is only feasible if a wide range of products is manufactured, the quantity sold is large, or the value of the product is high. The motor industry frequently sets up franchised retailers who deal solely with one make of car. Their fortunes are closely associated with those of the company and they have an incentive to sell the product. Part of the dealer's work is in provision of after-sales service, and firms may want to ensure that the quality is as high as possible. However, while manufacturers have expanded vertically into the distribution chain as far as the retail level, the more usual expansion is of the large retailer back to production, and bulk purchase from existing manufacturers for own-brand labels.

Small firms with fewer resources usually leave distribution to middlemen where a wider market can be serviced. Firms lacking marketing expertise may also leave distribution to the specialists. This may be the result of a decision to place the emphasis of the company on production and allow the marketing side of the operation to be controlled from outside the firm.

6.8.4 The Type of Middleman
The decision whether to use middlemen is affected by their availability to do the job required. They must be able to carry out those distribution activities which the manufacturer cannot perform economically himself. There must be co-operation and understanding of requirements from both sides. Once the decision of a given distribution channel is taken, it is not always easy to change it, and accepted trade practice may limit the choice in the first place. Thus the middleman's attitude towards the manufacturer's policies must be favourable and flexible. If the manufacturer decides to alter his product or marketing policies he does not want to find himself up against a wholesaler who will no longer handle any of his products because he does not like the change.

There may not be suitable middlemen available to deal with a product either because the area covered is wrong or because the middleman is satisfied with existing brands he is processing. In this case the manufacturer has to persuade him to stock his product in competition with substitutes, which can be a costly way of setting up a distribution chain. The existence of several competing products in the middleman's range may make him unsuitable since there will be less incentive for him to push the firm's brand. In addition the middleman may demand an advertising commitment from the manufacturer before stocking the product. The goods he handles need to be of similar price and quality, because a product that does not fit into his range may well not be presented to the best outlets. Lastly, the credit standing of the middleman is important since it affects the credit services that can be passed on to retailer or customer, and this may alter final sales considerably. No manufacturer wishes to find himself with outstanding debts from a wholesaler or retailer who is bankrupt or is forced to delay payments because of financial difficulties.

6.9 Conclusion

The choice of distribution channel is determined by the manufacturer based on his constraints of finance and skill, by the market in terms of the buyers, their size and consequent bargaining strength and by the type of product and its image. Each of these factors, taken with the company objectives over control, must be considered if the product is to reach the market place in the desired state. Persuading retailers and wholesalers to stock a product may be more difficult than its manufacture, and the inherent risk in handling new ideas means that they may never be taken up. The introduction of canned baby foods was only achieved in America by the persistence of one man who had to persuade mothers to pressure the shops they used to handle the product. Marketing people felt there was no future for canned baby foods and the manufacturer had to concentrate the needs of mothers to create an effective pressure group.

Work Section

A. Revision Questions

A1 Define Distribution.

A2 How can distribution costs influence the advantages of mass production?

A3 What is the major objective of distribution for the organisation?

A4 What are two subsidiary objectives that influence the choice of distribution channels?

A5 List four factors that affect the choice of distribution channel.

A6 Suggest a typical distribution channel for consumer goods.

A7 What is the economic significance of the retailer?

A8 How has the change in retailing patterns affected the control the manufacturer has over his products?

A9 What is the importance of the retailer to the manufacturer as part of overall sales policy?

A10 How and why does the distribution of industrial products differ from consumer goods?

A11 What are the services provided by middlemen?

A12 What competitive forces occur in the distribution channel?

B. Exercises/Case Studies

B1 What types of distribution channel would you select for the following products, and why?

a. Bottled beer

b. A radio alarm clock

c. Fresh vegetables

d. Household furniture

e. A complex piece of industrial pumping gear.

B2 Paraffin is an unpleasant product to handle although it is a cheap form of heating. At one time distribution was via agents who wholesaled to hardware stores and garages. However, sales fell with the change to self-service petrol stations and fewer stores continued to stock the product. Eventually delivery vehicles to supply customers directly were introduced by distribution agents, although they were costly to operate.

   Show the distribution channels employed and explain why you think sales of paraffin have continued to fall.

B3 Hobbihouse and Handiman are two new firms in the 'do-it-yourself market and they serve the same region. Independently, both companies have developed a new product for filling walls. Hobbihouse has decided to leave the distribution to the local wholesaler who has good contact with the relevant retail outlets. The wholesaler, who charges a mark-up of 15 per cent, has already agreed to handle the product and he has told Hobbihouse that he thinks it will have a reasonable chance of success, although the market is very price conscious. Handiman decided to cut out the wholesaler and sell direct to DIY retailers. The retailer mark-up is 33 per cent. Handiman's ex-factory price is set at £1.30 per pack while Hobbihouse has set its price ex-factory at £1.20 per pack.

    a. Assuming that production costs and unit profit are the same for both companies, why do you think Handiman is charging 10p per pack more than Hobbihouse?

    b. What will be the final price for each product when sold to the customer?

    c. Which company do you think has chosen the most suitable distribution channel, and why?

B4 A small but well-established firm has just developed a new amplifier which has performed well in tests and received good reviews in the hi-fi press. It is trying to decide how to distribute the product. Competitors sell their amplifiers through wholesalers and also direct to retailers, if the order size is big enough. Naturally, they use their own sales force to get orders directly from retailers, and some also visit the shops which buy from wholesalers. Any orders received are passed back to the wholesalers where appropriate. What are the advantages of each system of distribution and what method would you advise for the firm?

B5 A company manufacturing spray cans of paint for home car repairs has found a way of making metallic paint which matches existing colours more accurately than any other on the market. It estimates that there are around fourteen million cars on the road of which 10 per cent have metallic finishes. There are 200 wholesalers who handle spray paint products and 20,000 garages (largely owned by the major oil companies), 10,000 independent retailers and five car accessory chain stores. How would you advise the company to distribute the paint, explaining your reasons? Draw the distribution method you choose.

C. Essay Questions

C1 Why might a manufacturer be concerned to control the distribution of his product and how would he decide what channel to use?

C2 In what ways can a distribution channel hinder changes in products? How can a manufacturer help the middleman when he is introducing a new product?

C3 Explain why retailers have grown in size and comment on the shift in balance of power between retailers and manufacturers.

C4 'Middlemen are unnecessary additions to the job of distribution. They merely make products more expensive to the consumer'. Discuss.

Chapter 7

Advertising

Objective: *To show the extent of advertising and its importance to industry and services. To set out the structure of the advertising industry and to link advertising to the overall marketing plan of a company.*

Synopsis: *Advertising is intended to inform the market, and persuade consumers to use a particular product or service. As part of the marketing mix it must relate to the other aspects, contribute to the overall image and value of the product, and match the product's progress through the product life cycle. There are many forms of advertising, but the main emphasis of the chapter is on Manufacturers' Consumer Advertising. The structure of advertising involves the advertiser, the agency and the media. It is up to the advertiser to set the objectives and decide on the overall expenditure. The other elements design and carry the message. Controls exist to prevent the exploitation of the consumer.*

Plan of the chapter:

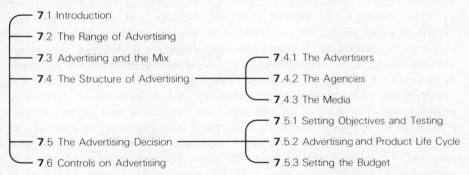

7.1 Introduction

7.2 The Range of Advertising

7.3 Advertising and the Mix

7.4 The Structure of Advertising
- **7**.4.1 The Advertisers
- **7**.4.2 The Agencies
- **7**.4.3 The Media

7.5 The Advertising Decision
- **7**.5.1 Setting Objectives and Testing
- **7**.5.2 Advertising and Product Life Cycle
- **7**.5.3 Setting the Budget

7.6 Controls on Advertising

7.1 Introduction

'If a man write a better book, preach a better sermon, or make a better mouse-trap than his neighbour, tho' he builds his house in the woods, the world will make a beaten path to his door.' (attributed to Emerson)

If, indeed, it was ever the case that a product would sell itself, it certainly is

not so now. With so many products available the problems of choosing between them are daunting enough, let alone discovering a new one by chance.
Producers need to communicate with the market to let them know what is
available and what special characteristics their product can offer which distin-
guishes it from everything else. This is as true for the trade as it is for the final
consumer. The need for information has led to the growth of advertising,
which is largely a one-way communication, and selling, which allows for feedback. This chapter looks at advertising, while Chapter 9 considers selling and
sales policy.

7.2 The range of advertising

'An advertisement is a paid-for communication intended to inform and/or
influence one or more people.' This definition of an advertisement was given
by Jeremy Bullmore, Chairman of J. Walter Thompson, London, which is
part of one of the largest advertising agencies in the world. It underlines the
breadth of advertising and what it attempts to achieve. Many people tend to
think of advertising in terms of television commercials and posters for consumer products, but the range is much wider. In addition to **display advertising** for consumer products, newspapers and magazines carry large classified
sections where individuals advertise for goods that they want, or offer things
for sale. St Valentine's day sees another sort of advertisement, placed where it
will reach a large audience, but intended for one person. There is also a large
block of advertising for the trade, placed in journals which reach a specific
group of people. Often these magazines are sent direct to those involved; for
example, *Grocer's Weekly* for the retail grocers trade. In recent years there has
been a sizeable growth in Government advertising. This includes Services
recruitment; information for the public about changes in policy as they affect
individuals and firms; exhortations to make the most efficient use of resources
as in the 'Save it' energy conservation programmes; and attempts to raise the
health of the nation by discouraging smoking and underlining the dangers of
drinking and driving. A quick perusal of the business section in the 'serious'
national newspapers will reveal financial advertising providing information on
share issues, the loan and investment of money and abbreviated company
accounts. Charities advertise to raise funds, pressure groups advertise to
encourage their view of the ideal political order, or the dangers to the environment. Large companies occasionally advertise in an attempt to improve
their corporate image. The list is endless, but it does show that there is much
more to advertising than the sale of detergents.

7.3 Advertising and the Mix

Advertising alone rarely sells a product, although there has recently been a significant increase in direct selling off the page, especially in the colour supplements. Usually advertising is closely linked with other aspects of the mix and is no substitute for the work of the sales force. Some advertising is wasteful in that it inevitably reaches a far wider audience than is necessary, but it has the advantage of being a cheaper form of communication for mass markets than individual selling. Combined with other aspects of sales promotion, it can make a valuable contribution. Yet good advertising cannot sell a poor product. It may achieve a first-time trial, but if the customer is not satisfied he is unlikely to try it again, and word soon gets round that the product is not worth purchasing. Should the product be one of a range of branded goods, the disappointment with one failure can create a refusal to purchase other products manufactured by the same firm. This, in itself, is an incentive for firms to ensure that their advertising is honest, although only certain aspects of the product may be stressed. There are also legal and voluntary controls which restrict the claims an advertiser may make. (See section 7.6.)

To be effective, advertising must pick out the special characteristics of a product and emphasise them. In this way the product is differentiated from its competitors because it embraces something unique. It is not always easy to create that specialness, but failure to do so means that advertising works at product rather than brand level and any expenditure by one firm may help competitors as well. Sometimes packaging is almost the only way to discriminate between makes of similar products. Advertising must concentrate on this aspect, familiarising the market with package design. With a well-structured campaign, seeing a package on the shelves of a supermarket should remind the buyer of the advertising and encourage a purchase. Thus advertising must link the product as it appears in a shop with the benefits suggested in the advertisement. Some products are more susceptible to advertising because their purchase depends as much on emotional factors as rational decisions. When we buy a product we are buying something that will fulfil a need. Cars can transport us from one place to another in more or less comfort, and with greater or less reliability. But there is an enormous mystique attached to the purchase of a car. This is emphasised by the time and concern spent over the decision, often much greater than over purchasing a house! Look at some advertisements for cars. You will see that when you buy a car you are getting more than the physical properties of a machine to move you around. A car is seen by many as a status symbol and the model you buy will tell everyone something about you. Each major manufacturer creates an image of his product through his advertising. Thus BMW has worked hard to build itself a position as a maker of cars for discerning and exclusive people – the price tag enhances this. Lancia has promoted its cars under the flag of 'The Most Italian Car' with all that the image of Italy suggests to the British market. Different manufacturers stress different aspects of their cars. A car that is just right for family motoring – solid, reliable and down to earth – is appealing to a different market from a sports car. Manufacturers of perfumes stress a particular style with which they associate their product – exclusive, outrageous, sexual. But perfumes are simply chemical liquids that smell. By association they offer the 'promise' of better things or an enhanced image, and this is what sells them.

Mass production requires a large market. Advertising is one of the ways of informing people about products and persuading them to buy. Naturally, not all products require the same level of advertising. A sophisticated piece of industrial machinery will not be 'sold' by advertising. The job of the sales force is much more important in explaining the merits of one piece of equipment against another. But while the selling can be effective in that situation, the cost of seeing individual customers of mass-produced consumer goods would be prohibitive – and often would be counter-productive since people do not want to be pestered about everything they buy. Advertising is the only way to communicate with a mass market, and it plays a very important part in keeping demand high enough to enable economies of scale to be passed on to the consumer in the form of lower prices. Figure 7.1 presents a diagrammatic picture of the importance of advertising and salesmen for different categories of product.

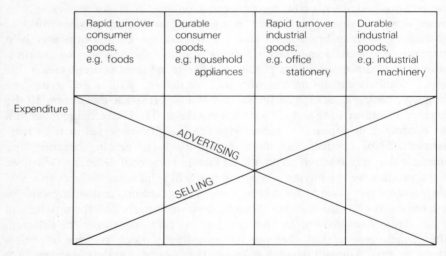

Fig. 7.1: Relative importance of selling and advertising in terms of expenditure

(*Source*: Smallbone: *The Practice of Marketing*, p. 268, Staples Press)

7.4 The Structure of Advertising

Manufacturers' Consumer Advertising (MCA), that is advertising of consumer goods by manufacturers, represents by far the largest share of all the types of advertising – 41 per cent of the total in 1978 – with classified at 21.9 per cent and retail advertising at 16.7 per cent. Expenditure on advertising as a whole represented 1.3 per cent of GNP in 1978.[1] (GNP is a measure of total expenditure on goods and services in the economy.) This gives some indication of the importance of advertising in the economy, yet it is a relatively recent phenomenon. The first advertisement is though to have been a papyrus of around 1,000 BC, advertising for a runaway slave. However, little was done until the end of the nineteenth century when Harmsworth brought out the first mass-circulation, popular newspaper, *The Daily Mail*. The publication of this paper, like others, relied heavily on expenditure by advertisers. The greater the extent of advertising the lower could be the cost to the reader, and within four years of its launch *The Daily Mail* had a circulation of one million. This followed the Education Acts of the late nineteenth century which began to set up basic education in England and significantly increased literacy. Combined with the greater national wealth produced by the Industrial Revolution, mass demand was encouraged by advertising and the basis for mass production of consumer goods was founded.

There are usually three groups involved in advertising. Firstly, the advertiser who pays for the advertisement and provides the overall brief in terms of objectives. Secondly, the agency, employed to design the advertisement, produce copy and select space, and often to co-ordinate the whole marketing strategy of a company. Thirdly, the media where the advertisement will appear.

7.4.1 The Advertiser

The reason for most advertising is to encourage sales of a product or service. It is only one of the forces that affects sales and must be integrated with the rest of the mix. The DAGMAR communications spectrum (see Fig. 7.2) represents the consumer stages between unawareness and action and the forces acting on those stages. It illustrates the need for continued advertising as the market changes, and its importance in reinforcing the consumer's purchase. In many cases there may be a block before action, as a result of brand loyalty which prevents the consumer from switching brands.

Many new products are launched each year, and the attention of the buyer has to be gained. Until this is achieved it is impossible to tell the potential of the product in sales terms. Only after the consumer is aware of the product's existence can he make a choice of whether to buy or not and later repurchase. For completely new ideas, the market may need 'educating' about how the product works and what it will do; for a new brand, greater emphasis will be put on the special characteristics which distinguish it from competitors' brands. For many household requirements, consumers use existing products and new variations have to be presented in such a way that the customer feels he is not taking too great a risk in trying something different. Launching a new product is a major undertaking and advertising is necessary to encourage a

---

[1] Advertising Association.

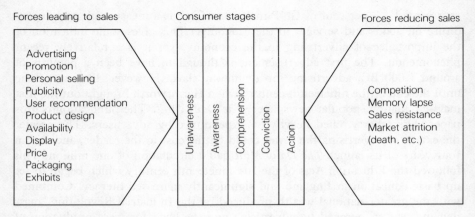

Fig. 7.2: DAGMAR communications spectrum

quick 'take-up' by the market. However, national advertising is very expensive; perhaps up to £.2.5 m. for the launch of a new cigarette. Failure of the product to live up to expectations means that all the production and marketing effort will be wasted.

As the costs of the launch escalate, so manufacturers have become much more cautious. Where feasible, test markets are run to discover market reaction and minimise the cost of failure. This is not possible for products whose life cycle is very short, such as fashion goods, nor for products where fixed costs are high and the technicalities of production mean that whole mass production lines must be set up. However, as with products, advertisements are often tested to see what sort of response they create. For products which are test marketed in particular regions, advertising is part of the process, but not all products will fit easily into a regional launch. Those with a relatively small market, such as expensive, prestige goods, require national advertising with a national market to ensure sufficient sales for profitable production. Even so, both product and advertising will be checked in some way.

When a product is modified as a result of a technical change, a new use, or simply restyled, advertising is needed to inform the market of the change. However, it is unlikely that it will need to be as intensive as for a new product and there is less need for test marketing, although different advertising copy may be tested by consumer panels.

The bulk of manufacturers' consumer advertising is not concerned with launching new products, but in the promotion of existing goods and service, some of which have been around for years. This advertising often draws criticism for being wasteful and adding to the cost of goods. However, it is a necessary part of the marketing process if sales of products are to remain high and the maturity stage of the product life cycle is to be lengthened.

With any communication we tend to filter out those parts which do not seem relevant to our needs. Advertisements are easily forgotten and then they cease to help sell the product. How many advertisements can you remember from last month? How many can you partially remember without being certain what product was being promoted? In order to keep the product at the forefront of buyers' minds, continued advertising programmes are necessary.

The relevance of the communication also dictates the need for constant advertising as markets change and new consumers come into the picture. At thirteen you may not be very interested in advertisements for cars, but by the time you are in your twenties, you want to become more aware of what is available and you will be attuned to car advertisements. What they say has become relevant to your needs. Furniture advertising may not excite you now and consequently you will tend to filter out such advertisements, but as soon as you set up your own home they will have a greater impact. Much advertising of existing products can be justified by the need to keep in touch with the changing markets. It also reassures those who have already purchased the product.

Advertising can affect the rate of use of a product. This is particularly true of television and radio commercials which may remind the consumers to make use of the product. A butter commercial transmitted in the evening is not going to cause people to rush out and buy there and then, although it may help make their minds up about what brand they will buy next day. However, it may have the immediate effect of suggesting a piece of buttered toast and so increase the use of the product; a beer commercial may encourage you to take a can from the kitchen.

Advertising actually alters the 'perceived' nature of the product by giving it a particular image, so enhancing its value to the consumer. It may seem unethical to build up an aura around a product, but if the product becomes more attractive it increases its value to the consumer who feels an emotional response to it. For products such as cornflakes or washing powders, creating the image is part of the process of distinguishing one brand from another and building up a brand loyalty. By showing the product in agreeable surroundings, the product becomes acceptable and customers feel secure because they can relate to the way it has been presented. Thus a particular hair shampoo is 'right' because it is used by fashionable/comfortable/easy-going people, and that is its image. One problem faced by Rowntrees in the early stages of its launch of 'Matchmakers' was a failure to link the product to a clear market. There was no definite identity for people to relate to, and yet to establish the brand Rowntrees had to show the segment of the market for which Matchmakers were designed. For luxury items this is even more important. Buying a Mercedes or a Jaguar brings with it much more than a means of travel. It fulfils emotional needs about status and quality, and advertising plays an important part in creating the exclusiveness that these cars have.

Our impressions of products are easily affected by the promotion and packaging that surrounds them. Consider packing Marmite in a toothpaste tube (with toothpaste tube lettering) or Remy Martin cognac in a washing-up liquid bottle and you will see the impact this has on the desirability of the product.

Thus packaging affects the value we attach to a product and if we want to feel 'special' it is no use wearing perfume or after-shave from a jam jar.

Retailer advertising is a rather different operation. With the exception of the national chains such as Tesco or Sainsburys, there is little television or national newspaper advertising because it would be wasteful in terms of the coverage gained and the geographic requirements of the market. Most retailer advertising is strictly local and places great emphasis on price. Even the national chains advertise in this way because there is greater flexibility. Copy does not have to be produced far in advance, and different regions may offer different prices as stock levels and purchases vary. Because retailer advertising is so price conscious, there are frequent changes as new situations develop, and the local press is best suited to deal with these.

7.4.2 The Agencies

In the nineteenth century (as now) advertising was a major source of revenue for newspapers. Specialist services grew to co-ordinate the sale of advertising space and the buyers for it. These specialists were the agencies who acted as brokers for the newspapers, and although paid a **commission** by the papers, they began to develop links with the advertisers by providing services for them. The agencies saw that the way to maintain the loyalty of advertisers was to become expert in advising on the types of space and publication best suited to the needs of the product. This grew into assistance in the creation of the copy and finally agencies took over the design of advertisements. Expertise in the creation of advertisements and the cross-fertilisation of ideas between different products meant that the agencies could offer services and skills the advertisers could not match. Competition between the agencies grew and the newspapers began to organise the agency business. It was in the interests of the media to encourage good advertising because successful promotions meant more space sold. The media are paid by the advertiser, via the agency which retains a commission for its services. The agencies were made responsible for payment for the space taken in the media and they have to collect the money from the advertisers. In this way the media are relieved of the job of checking out the financial position of advertisers. Media buying is very complex, and recently several media-buying agencies have grown up.

The agencies provide services for the media and the advertiser. They are generally independent organisations, unaffiliated to any manufacturing company. It is their job to see that copy is delivered to the media on time, in the correct form for printing and transmitting, and that it is suitable for the medium and its image. For their clients, agencies advise on the type of space available and the media best suited to the desired market. They aim to achieve relevant coverage at the lowest cost. In addition to creating and producing the advertisements, agencies offer a wide range of services which are paid for direct by the advertiser. Often they advise on the total marketing strategy for a company and co-ordinate the various parts of the 'mix' to produce a unified approach to the product.

The choice of agency is in the hands of the manufacturer. It may not always pay to choose a large agency because, although the breadth of expertise may be present, the client company may not receive as much personal attention of the agency's top talent as it would from a smaller agency; similarly a massive advertising programme may be too large an undertaking for a small agency and the firm will use one of the bigger ones. Usually the choice is made after several presentations have been made by different agencies, although making a judgement between them may involve much more than a purely financial decision. Agencies have to work closely with their clients and personalities are important.

7.4.3 The Media

The media refer to the places where advertisements can be displayed, and include the press and magazines, television and radio, billboards both by the road, on stations or on moving vehicles such as trains, buses, lorries and vans. Almost all advertising requires a mass media; even recruitment advertising may need wide coverage to obtain the best selection of candidates from which to make an appointment.

		Per cent of total Advertising Expenditure	
	£ m. 1978	*1960*	*1978*
Press	1,236	70.9	67.4
Television	482	22.3	26.3
Poster and Transport	68	5.0	3.7
Cinema	13	1.5	0.7
Radio	35	0.3	1.9

Fig. 7.3: UK advertising and expenditure by media

(*Source*: AA)

Figure 7.3 shows that the press makes up by far the largest proportion of the total, and the growth of regional papers accounts for most of the increasing expenditure. Radio advertising has grown markedly since the introduction of independent local radio in 1974. The decline in cinema advertising reflects the decline in audiences.

The choice of media will depend on the product, the market for which it is intended and the finance available. Advertisers seek to communicate to the largest number of people in the relevant market at the lowest cost. Thus circulation figures, readership surveys and cost information are indispensable to the advertiser. Much of this information can be obtained from British Rate and Data (BRAD) which is published monthly. Circulation figures are compiled by the Audit Bureau of Circulations (ABC), an independent body measuring the 'sold circulation' of all publications that subscribe to it. It was set up to prevent fraudulent circulation figures from being published and it handles more than 1,600 publications. Some publications do not belong to the ABC, often for reasons of small circulation or where figures are not particularly important (e.g. some local publications), but advertisers tend to be wary of figures which are not independently certified.

National dailies	ABC circulation figures[1]	Readers per copy	Single column centimetre rate[2]	Full page standard rate
Daily Express	2,405,638	2.8	£40[3]	£9,250[3]
Daily Mail	1,946,058	2.7	£28	£7,056
Daily Mirror	3,616,099	3.1	£248[4]	£14,740
Daily Star	937,866[5]	3.0[5]	£11	£2,700
Daily Telegraph	1,493,827	2.5	£25	£10,650[3]
Financial Times	204,608	3.6	£19.50	£8,736
The Guardian	388,304	3.2	£20	£9,000
The Sun	3,805,575	3.1	£45	£10,710
The Times	295,059[6]	2.9[6]	£20	£8,960
Sundays				
News of the World	4,642,585	2.7	£47	–
The Observer	1,162,980	3.0	£22	£10,000
Sunday Express	3,231,734	2.6	£56	£21,800
Sunday Mirror	3,870,974	3.0	£224[4]	£13,200
Sunday People	3,925,522	2.8	£43	£11,500
Sunday Telegraph	1,267,336	2.7	£19	£8,500
The Sunday Times	1,399,073[6]	2.6[6]	£35	£15,680

[1] Average figures Jan. – Dec. 1979 relating to UK and Eire.
[2] Min. 3 scc.
[3] Rates for Mon. – Fri.
[4] ⅛th column
[5] based on Apr. – June 1979
[6] Jan. – Dec. 1978.

Fig. 7.4: Circulation figures and standard charges (Rates as at April 1980)
(*Source*: BRAD, ABC)

Figure 7.4 shows the circulation of some of the major daily and Sunday papers, together with standard charges for space. In addition to this basic rate there are supplementary charges dependent on the position of the advertisement. Thus front page, next to special feature articles, and 'solus' position where only one advertisement occurs on a page, attract higher rates. The 'single column centimetre' is the usual unit from which other charges are calculated. It refers to the cost of one centimetre of length in one column of the paper.

The advertiser usually leaves the choice of media to the agency whose job it is to submit the advertisement, sometimes specifying the page and position. As a rough yardstick, comparative circulations are based on the cost per 1,000 circulation. For example, the cost per 1,000 circulation of a single column centimetre taken in the *Daily Express* is:

$$\frac{\text{cost}}{\text{circulation}} \times 1,000 = \frac{£40}{2,405,638} \times 1,000 = £0.0167$$

compared to *The Times* at £0.068. You can calculate the others from Fig. 7.4. Cost is not the only important factor, and although it is about four times as expensive to advertise in *The Times* as the *Daily Express*, the nature of the market may make the former a more desirable paper to use for a particular product.

Not all publications can be costed in quite the same way as newspapers because some have far more readers per copy than others. A single copy of *Punch* is likely to be read by more than one person and also to be around for much longer than a newspaper. For example, waiting rooms for doctors and dentists often have a pile of past issues and so they are seen by a large number of people. Weeklies such as the *Radio Times* or *Newsweek* also receive lengthy perusal and magazines serve different groups of consumers. There is little use in advertising children's clothes in *Farmers' Weekly* or office machinery in *Vogue*. The advertiser needs to know how many people in the relevant market are likely to see his advertisement, and for this he wants a breakdown of the readers by socio-economic class, occupation, age, sex and so on. To gather this information, the advertising industry undertakes continuous market research; the Joint Industry Committee for National Advertising Readership Surveys (JICNARS) is the source of information on consumer profile and readership per copy of each publication. The survey, of around 15,000 people, is taken every six months to provide the information and it gives advertisers a clear idea of cost per reader and the market served by each publication. A few examples are given in Fig. 7.5.

From this information the advertiser can calculate the cost per reader for each publication. Specialist magazines tend to be more expensive than those with a general circulation. From the advertiser's point of view this does not necessarily make them less attractive because those who take the publication may closely approximate the relevant market.

Similar surveys exist for radio and television coverage and for cinema audiences. As with commercial radio, posters and the regional press, commercial television is regional and thus advertisers are able to limit their promotion by geographic area. This is very important if their market or their message differs between regions, and for testing both product and commercial in one area before launching nationally. There are thirteen regions and each has a different

Publication	ABC circula-tion	Average readers per copy	Sex Men (%)	Women (%)	Class Profile ABC₁ (%)	C₂DE (%)
Cosmopolitan	475,306	3.5	30	70	59	41
Economist	67,341	7.8	75	25	84	16
Exchange & Mart	475,306	8.1	74	26	41	59
Practical Householder	124,182	10.5	66	34	46	54
Punch	68,055	13.2	69	31	72	28
Radio Times	3,664,969	2.7	47	53	50	50
TV Times	3,648,655[1]	2.9	45	55	41	59
Vogue	105,853	18.2	20	80	59	41
Woman's Own	1,563,807	3.6	19	81	41	59

[1] January to June 1979

Fig. 7.5: Circulation, readership and consumer profile

(*Source*: JICNARS NRS January-December 1979.)

coverage with costs linked to the number of households reached. For example, London Weekend covers 4.4 m. households and a 30-second peak time spot costs £9,000[1]; ATV covers 3.2 m. households and a similar spot costs £5,200; Yorkshire Television covers 2.2 m. households with a rate of £4,100; Channel reaches less than 0.5 m. households and the rate is £56 for a peak time 30-second spot.

As with advertisements placed in special positions in papers or magazines, there are surcharges and discounts for different requirements. The cheapest 30-second spot on Thames Television costs £340[1] and is transmitted up to 4 p.m. Obviously the audience is smaller and of a different composition to peak rate time from 6.45 p.m. to 10.15 p.m. Commercial radio is a significantly cheaper medium through which to advertise. Thirty seconds on Capital Radio during prime time costs £340 at basic rate with reductions for contract advertising. In addition, the costs of producing a radio commercial are much lower than for television or the cinema. However, certain products are particularly suited to one medium rather than other. Colour, for example, can be effective for advertising food. Movement may be important for visual impact.

Guaranteeing a particular spot for a commercial attracts a varying surcharge. Discounts are given on volume advertising and seasonal conditions. In the summer television viewing is well down on winter months and the rates vary accordingly.

[1] All rates as at April 1980. *Source*: JICTAR and BRAD.

With the exception of advertisements at stations or in buses and trains where there is a captive audience receptive to detailed information, poster advertising relies for its effectiveness on a single short message which can be quickly understood as people pass by. Obviously, the number of posters, their size and positon are important in communicating the advertiser's message to a large audience. Ten sites per 100,000 population may achieve 75 per cent coverage, but most of the best sites are taken by advertisers who use them for all-year-round campaigns, so this medium is used by relatively few firms.

Media	Advantages	Disadvantages
Newspapers	Low cost/high coverage Reader can refer back. Authority, derived from newspaper's standing. Can be linked to relevant feature articles. (Regional newspapers good for local campaigns and test markets but cost per readership higher.)	No movement or sound. Relatively poor reproduction quality. Plenty of space often necessary to achieve impact.
Magazines	Colour. Specific readership, especially in specialist magazines. Reader can refer back. Authority derived from magazine's standing. Can be linked to relevant feature articles.	Not very flexible because of time required for printing. No sound or movement. Plenty of space often required to achieve impact.
Television	High coverage. Colour. Movement and sound. Can show how product works. Easy to gain interest.	Expensive. Viewer cannot refer back. Little flexibility for change of advertisements.
Posters	High coverage. Colour. High 'glance' readership.	Effects on sales difficult to monitor. Limited information about product.

Fig. 7.6: Summary of advantages and disadvantages of the four main types of media

7.5 The Advertising Decision

As with other elements in the mix, there is a clear decision-making theme surrounding the choice of advertising. Often the agency is a major source of information for the advertiser, and experience of different campaigns means that it can provide an overall marketing strategy for a product. The type of product, the nature of the market and the finance available all influence the decision as well as the overall objectives of the company with regard to its product range. Competitors' actions are important and heavy advertising on their part may require a similar response to keep each brand in the forefront of consumers' minds.

7.5.1 Setting Objectives and Testing

Although much of the detail of advertising can be left for the agency to decide, it is vital that a clear brief is given. This involves setting out the objectives of the campaign and the financial constraints governing how much money is available to promote a product or range of products. There should be an agreed method of testing the results, remembering that advertising is only one of many factors affecting the overall sales performance. In a declining market, a good campaign might hold the sales level constant, whereas in a situation where the market is buoyant sales might rise in spite of poor promotion. This could lead to a false sense of security which will be rudely shattered when conditions turn against the product.

As already explained, one of the purposes of advertising is to inform, and it is possible to test the success of this by surveying the knowledge of the product before and after a campaign. Clarity is essential in the communication, if people are to understand it. An advertisement has to compete with both those of direct competitors, and other products for the consumer's attention. Boredom, conflicting claims and other advertisements all constitute '**noise**' which reduces the effectiveness of a campaign, so distinctiveness and interest are all-important. However, there is a danger that the style (e.g. humour) of an advertisement will be remembered rather than the product it is trying to promote. The product must always be the hero.

The awareness that is created by advertising must be favourable. The launch of the Strand cigarette has become a famous case of 'getting it wrong'. The commercial, which was beautifully made and won a variety of awards, depicted a man, clad in a raincoat, walking at night along a deserted London street in the rain with the caption, 'You are never alone with a Strand'. Whilst awareness of the product was quickly achieved, sales collapsed because the advertisement reminded people of all the worst parts of cigarette smoking – anti-social, downtrodden, ignored and suicidal. Advertising of 'Persil', however, has been consistently successful. It shows the consumer as a mother who is concerned about the whiteness of Persil for her whole family, as part of her overall care, in a socially neutral situation. People want to associate themselves with such an image, and hence the product, because they see it as an 'ideal'.

Attitude surveys help provide information on how consumers view a product, and detailed research is carried out on the various qualities they feel it possesses. For example, a deodorant soap might be compared with other brands and consumers asked whether it was effective, had a masculine smell, appeared expensive or cheap, and so on. With responses ranked on a ten-point scale from one extreme to the other (effective 10, ineffective 0) a profile of attitudes towards the product can be constructed.

Advertising is not only directed at the consumer. A manufacturer may have to show that he is building up the market by undertaking an advertising campaign in order to persuade retailers and wholesalers to handle the product or increase their stocks. The advertiser also has to show the trade the advantages of selling the product, and this may well involve emphasis on attributes which are different from those the consumer expects. Size, packaging, discounts and special offers to middlemen are likely to increase the enthusiasm with which they push the product, and so improve sales.

7.5.2 Advertising and the Product Life Cycle

The position of the product in the product life cycle influences the kind of advertising used to promote it. During the development stage, the emphasis is on telling the market about the product and showing the benefits of using it. Once into the growth stage the emphasis switches away from the product to the brand as loyalties are built up to compete with imitative products. It becomes important to persuade the consumer to be more selective and to buy one brand rather than another. The market is aware of the product and so more time can be spent on building an image and creating an emotional response to one particular brand. This intensifies through maturity, and extension strategies enhance the distinctiveness of the brand. Decline either calls for more advertising or a different strategy, to enable one brand to increase its share at the expense of the others, or a reduction in advertising as the product is phased out.

7.5.3 Setting the Budget

Advertising costs money and it is important that it is well spent. Generally, in a competitive market where the main manufacturers are heavy advertisers, the cost of promotion can act as an effective deterrent to new firms entering the market. The difference in media costs means that the choice of advertising is partly determined by the money available. However, setting the budget is notoriously difficult. There are several common methods although each has its drawbacks.

1. The budget can be set as a percentage of past sales. Although this has the advantage of using finance that has already been earned, it does not take the future market into consideration, or the pressures from competition. Growth in sales is not supported by extra spending, and a decline in sales is not reversed by increasing advertising. Each year expenditure falls, and with it market share.

2. A percentage of expected sales in the forthcoming year allows greater flexibility and takes into consideration changes in the position of the company with regard to the market. However, if sales do not reach targets the company may find itself in financial difficulty, and reduce its allocation in subsequent years.

3. The advertising budget can be calculated on the amount that competitors are likely to spend. While this does allow an assessment of the market, it can lead to competitive advertising. Then each firm spends more and more in response to the amount of advertising in the market as a whole. Very high expenditure on advertising makes the entry of new firms into the market more difficult, unless they have enormous financial resources behind them.

7.6 Controls on Advertising

Advertising is frequently criticised for misleading and exploiting the consumer, pushing him into buying goods that he does not want, and saddling him with desires which he cannot fulfil. Such a view places a pretty low value on the intelligence of the consumer. It is true that the purpose of advertising is to inform and persuade, and if no one acted differently after seeing an advertisement there would be no point in spending vast sums of money promoting products. The benefits of mass production, in terms of low cost and thus low prices, can only occur if there is a mass market. Advertising is part of the process of creating and maintaining that market, by providing information and showing products to their best advantage. Products are presented in attractive terms to encourage people to buy them, and to enhance their value to the consumer. This does not mean that their presentation is misleading. Clearly, the consumer needs protection from false descriptions and claims and certain types of consumer deserve greater protection than others. Thus there are strict codes applying to advertisements for children's products and also for products that can be harmful, such as cigarettes and drink.

The consumer is protected from dishonest and offensive advertisements by law and the advertising industry. There are many statutes governing advertising but the most important is the Trade Descriptions Act 1968 which laid down that the contents of an advertisement constituted a Trade Description, and anyone involved with the advertisement could be prosecuted if it could be shown that the claims made for the product or the description were false. Individuals can complain to their local Inspector of Weights and Measures, who would prosecute if there was a bona fide case to make. Clearly some advertising, such as Heineken ('refreshes the parts other beers cannot reach'), is not making a serious claim for the product and can be seen not to be trying to mislead the consumer. The Trade Descriptions Act also laid down the conditions where special price or sale price offers may apply. To qualify for a special price the product must have been sold at the higher price for at least twenty-eight days continuously, in the previous six months.

The Independent Broadcasting Authority, set up in 1973, is empowered by statute to control advertising on radio and television. It vets all advertisements submitted for broadcasting and checks the facts and method of presentation. About one third of all commercials have to be amended, either because they might mislead the public or because they do not conform to the IBA code on advertising standards and practice. All advertisements must be 'legal, decent, honest and truthful' and this opening statement of the code is the criterion used to judge broadcast advertising.

In addition to legal controls and the IBA, the industry has its own voluntary body to monitor advertising. The Advertising Standards Authority, financed by a 0.1 per cent levy on all non-broadcast advertising, operates the British Code of Advertising Practice. It is a detailed document prescribing in the introduction that '... advertisements should be legal, decent, honest and truthful, ... prepared with a sense of responsibility to the consumer, ... conform to the principles of fair competition as generally accepted in business. ...' The media will not handle any advertisement that contravenes the code, or is under examination by the ASA, and as such the code acts as strong deterrent to unsuitable advertisements. In addition, the ASA, which relies on public reaction to, and complaints about, advertisements, publishes reports of companies under investigation. Advertisers are keen to avoid public censure and the code is effective in maintaining standards.

Work Section

A. Revision Questions

A1 List five categories of advertising.

A2 What two functions does advertising perform?

A3 For what category of goods is advertising most heavily used?

A4 What are the three groups involved in advertising?

A5 List the five consumer stages in the DAGMAR communications spectrum.

A6 Why is the major part of MCA concerned with existing products?

A7 How can advertising add value to a product?

A8 What is the job of an advertising agency?

A9 What are the advantages and disadvantages of television as an advertising medium?

A10 How does advertising alter as a product passes through the stages of the product life cycle?

A11 List three methods of setting an advertising budget.

A12 What are the main controls on advertising?

B. Exercises/Case Studies

B1 Using Fig. 7.4, calculate the cost per 1,000 circulation of a single column centimetre for the *Sun* and the *Daily Telegraph*. Would you necessarily choose the lower cost paper to advertise a product? Give reasons for your answer.

B2 Compare the readership of *Vogue* and *Cosmopolitan*. What does the information contained in Fig. 7.5 tell an advertiser trying to decide which publication to use? Would the larger circulation of *Woman's Own* make it a more satisfactory publication in which to advertise a beauty product?

B3 Mustard is an easily forgotten product. Colman's has always had the major share of the market and it developed the product from a powder which had to be mixed with water, to a ready-mixed convenience food packed in tubes and jars. It introduced a range of three new flavours (French, German and American) to its existing English mustard as a way of increasing market penetration. Market research showed that sales expanded and that customers were buying more mustard rather than merely switching flavours. However, American mustard, which was relatively mild, did not sell well. Colman's sales of all mustards fell 2% between 1977 and mid-1978. This was partly the result of a nine-month gap in advertising. As its advertising agency, what would you have suggested the company should do, and how would you have dealt with the American problem?

B4 The chart compares the retail price index for food with the price index of 65 heavily advertised food brands.
1. What are the implications of the chart for the advertiser?
2. What are the implications for the consumer?

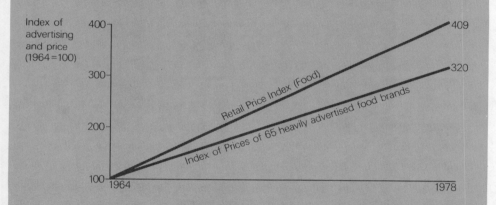

(*Source:* CSO, Shaw's Price List, AGB)

B5 The early stages of making a television commercial usually involve the construction of a 'storyboard' made up of rough sketches and words of the key scenes. These are tested with a group of consumers to obtain their reactions, and discussed with the advertiser. Once agreed, and refined, a film company will be commissioned to shoot the commercial. Since a television commercial rarely lasts longer than 60 seconds, every frame is vital. A 60-second commercial may have more than 76 'cuts' and yet the finished product must run smoothly. The whole process may take twelve weeks, or more. A finished black and white storyboard is reproduced on page 114. Examine the script and pictures and explain what each stage is trying to do, together with the significance of each frame.

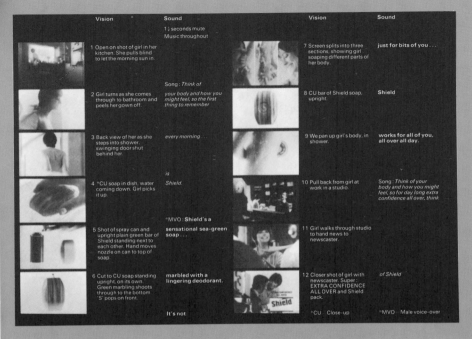

© Unilever. Reproduced with permission

C Essay Questions

C1 What factors might affect advertising strategy when launching new products?

C2 What factors should a firm consider when designing its advertising?

C3 How should a firm determine its expenditure on advertising in any period?

C4 Is advertising a waste of resources from the point of view of (a) a firm, and (b) the industry of which that firm is a member?

C5 'Advertising is a means of exploiting the consumer by forcing products on him that he does not want.' Discuss.

Chapter 8

Sales Policy and Sales Promotion

Objective: *To show the importance and function of the sales force. To explain sales promotion and its various forms and show how it can affect the sales performance of a company.*

Synopsis: *Selling is designed to communicate with buyers and persuade them to use a product. Like sales promotion, it operates at the point-of-sale and 'pushes' the product by emphasising its use and image. It needs to be closely linked with other parts of the mix to be as effective as possible.*

Plan of the chapter:

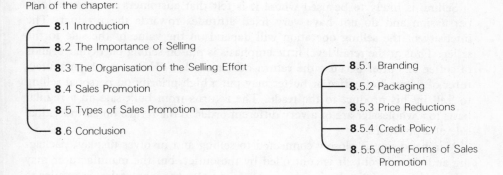
8.1 Introduction

In the last chapter we looked at advertising which is designed to inform and persuade. It works by demonstrating the advantages of a product and 'pulling' the consumer into a shop to buy. Sales policy covers the work of sales force selling a product into the trade or out to the consumer, and sales promotion which is designed to 'push' the product at the point-of-sale.

Unlike advertising, which is a general communication, selling deals with a specific target, presenting the product in a way most suitable for the particular needs of the buyer. The sales force is able to gauge the response and alter the sales pitch according to individual requirements. In the past, companies have tried to replace the sales force by advertising and providing an ordering service. However, experience shows that advertising does not replace the salesman's job; it merely reinforces, and successful companies run the two side by side. Selling is expensive because it is time-consuming but order books are much larger as a result of it. Typically, selling takes five to ten times as much of the overall marketing budget as advertising and the justification for this comes from the returns on that cost.

Sales policy plays its most important part at the time of purchase. Figure 8.1 shows the relative importance of advertising and sales promotion.

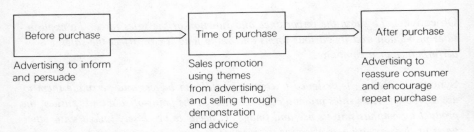

Fig. 8.1: The relative importance of advertising and selling

Selling is likely to be used where it is felt that customers are amenable to persuasion and do not have very fixed attitudes towards the product. The intensity of the selling operation will depend on the value of the sale to the seller. Thus at the retail level little emphasis is put on selling particular brands of coffee or butter because the return per unit is low. However, the manufacturer of a brand of coffee or butter may put a high priority on personal selling to 'sell in' his product to the trade. The returns from bulk sale on a regular basis to a wholesaler are of a very different order to the return on an individual sale of a product.

Merchandising is closely connected to selling and involves display, packaging and store layout. It is controlled by the outlet, but the manufacturer may offer assistance through his sales force. It is up to the wholesaler or retailer to make use of this, and often, when faced with masses of schemes from the makers of each of his brands, the chance of any particular scheme being accepted is small. For large companies this has led to the growth of separate merchandising experts who follow up salesman as part of the package provided by the manufacturer. Increasingly selling has involved fitting the product to the purchaser's needs, rather than just pushing the product. This requires an understanding of the operations of retailers and wholesalers and their differing objectives. For the manufacturer, selling primarily involves increasing the turnover of his particular brand and designing schemes to assist this. However, a retailer is interested in the total sales of many different products and any point-of-sale assistance is viewed in terms of the whole store. Advice on store layout and provision of display equipment is only likely to be accepted if it will lead to more customers using the outlet and a broad increase in purchases.

If the salesman is seen as a source of useful advice for the outlet he will be in a better position to sell since he can explain promotion schemes and how they will affect the store's performance. Working with the buyer will enable him to understand particular problems and, as far as possible, help in overcoming them. Hence he can check on the level of stock and its condition, suggest ways of improving the use of space and different possibilities for display that can show off both store and product to good advantage. If the salesman has a range of products to look after, armed with knowledge of the stock turnover for each item within the range, he can make sensible estimates of the needs of the buyer. It is not to the salesman's advantage to push products and quantities that the retailer will not be able to dispose of because, although it may give a high short-term sale for the company, repeat orders will be down and disenchantment with the firm may lead to the range being dropped in favour of another.

8.2 The Importance of Selling

For many retailers and small independent wholesalers the only direct personal contact with their suppliers comes through the visits of salesmen. This places an important burden on the salesman as he is the flag bearer for the company and his performance and personality can make the difference between securing an order and losing an outlet.

Communication of information concerning the product is an important part of the overall selling operation. The salesman present his products in a favourable light, pointing out their peculiar advantages. Because information passed down the channel of distribution tends to become distorted, the immediacy and urgency lost, the job of direct communication to all levels becomes more important. Rumours grow rapidly and may lead to expectations that cannot be fulfilled or antagonistic attitudes towards the manufacturer. The message that the salesman has to get across must be clear and also distinctive so that it stands out from that of competitors. Any promotion or display scheme has to fight for the buyer's interest and that places a special demand on the salesman. It must be relevant to the store for it to generate support and this is a prime objective.

As well as the means of communicating with the market, the salesman is an important source of information for the company. Because he is working closely with the distributors he is in a good position to find out what customer reaction is, and their views on the strengths and weaknesses of the product. Trade reaction is important because they have to handle the product and usually stock it in large quantity. Given the demands on space by different products, gimmicks which make sense to the company for promotion may be a severe disadvantage when it comes to selling.

The salesman is also uniquely positioned to see any trends in customer buying habits. If there is a reduction in sales through independent retailers, it may be that people are buying more in supermarkets. Thus the firm may want to redirect its selling approach. This can either be a general shift or one specific to a town where a new supermarket has just opened. Information on competitors' plans is also available. Salesmen can report back on any test markets or developments in competitors' products and the way they are selling them, as well as the market reaction. This grass roots information is vital in helping the firm to decide on new policies and new products. Sales information is also one method for the company to check on the performance of its sales staff and deal with any variation from the sales plan as soon as it arises.

8.3 The Organisation of the Selling Effort

The sales manager controls the overall selling effort. It is his job to organise the sales teams into effective units. Forecasts of sales and profits are based on the findings of market research. Annual sales targets are then set in consultation with the production and finance departments. The sales budget includes the cost of the selling operation, and from this the priorities for funds are decided. The sales manager has to decide the extent of selling necessary at each stage of the distribution channel. In some cases it will be more important to concentrate on wholesalers rather than retailers because the wholesaler may have his own well-developed sales team.

The annual sales target is broken down by area and market where quotas for each sales team are agreed. These quotas are later used as a yardstick for measuring performance. Each sales area must be examined independently because they each have different factors that influence sales. The important considerations are:

1. The density of the market. Where the market is concentrated, a sales team can cover more outlets. In a geographically dispersed market more time is taken in travelling.
2. The size of the outlet. Some sales areas will include buying offices for large wholesalers and national retail chains. The volume of sales will be greater for those sales forces than for those which have to service an area with many small retailers.
3. The regional charactertistics of market. Some areas cannot sustain the same level of demand as others. In areas of high unemployment, for example, the market for luxury goods is not as great as in London and the South East. Similarly, different regional tastes will affect the level of sales each salesman can achieve.
4. New markets. If the firm is developing a new market for its products more time will be taken to persuade the trade to handle the product and to help with setting up displays and promotions in the stores. Similarly, the launch of a new product will require extra selling time in all areas and this

requirement must be reflected in both manpower and financial planning.

5. Competitors' methods of selling. Where competitors employ large sales forces to sell into the trade, the firm may have to increase its own sales effort to ensure sufficient attention is paid to its products.
6. The complexity of the product. Technically complex products require more assistance from the sales staff, either to ensure that the trade can deal with the queries it receives from customers, or to provide their own back-up service
7. Special promotions. If the firm has decided to undertake special promotions such as demonstration of the product, the sales staff will have to spend more time with each outlet.

All of these factors affect the volume of sales that each team can achieve in a given time period.

Once the targets have been set the sales department has to organise the deployment of its sales force. Usually a salesman will have a pre-planned cycle of visits to carry out each month. **Operational research** has been an important tool in planning the best route to avoid wasted travel time, but the skill of the salesman is important too, for the length of each call will be affected by the buyer's commitments, and he may not always be immediately available when the salesman arrives. The frequency of calling depends on the type of product, and on the importance of the retailer or wholesaler to the company. Obviously an order for 50,000 units has a higher priority than one for 1,000 units. For most consumer goods a visit once every four to six weeks is about average.

The sales department has to organise major presentations for its sales staff to explain the company's objectives and the attributes of the products they are putting on the market. To be effective, the sales force must have a full understanding of product specifications and pricing, in addition to any special schemes that are being launched to help sell the products. These are followed up by detailed regional meetings where the job of each member is explained and difficulties ironed out. Debriefing sessions to gather feedback information are also the responsibility of the sales department.

Good selling requires enthusiasm and a belief in the value of both product and strength of the company. Understanding the buyer's point of view as well as the company needs can strain loyalties so motivation is all important.

There is a variety of ways in which the salesman is paid. Straight commission may provide a considerable incentive but it encourages the salesman to look to his short-term interests. These may conflict with the long-term requirements of the company and cause him to neglect the display and advice functions that do not directly lead to sales. Salary independent of sales may not provide sufficient motivation, although it gives the company more control over the job. Some combination of the two is becoming common practice, although commission is often difficult to allocate fairly because of the difference in opportunities presented by different products and regions.

8.4 Sales Promotion

Sales promotion covers most selling techniques which persuade and motivate people to buy at the point-of-sale. It is closely integrated with advertising, reminding the consumers of what they have seen and giving prominence to the product so that it will jog the memory and secure a purchase. It is the job of the sales force to communicate special promotions to the buyer if they are to have any effect.

The objective of sales promotion is to increase the manufacturer's sales. It can be achieved in any of the following ways:

- by encouraging new consumers to try the product, or existing ones to use it again;
- by increasing the number of outlets handling the product;
- by raising the level of consumer and distributor stocks.

The essence of sales promotion is to 'push' the product to the trade and consumer, and it can operate at any level in the distribution channel. Ultimately the rate of stock turn is dependent on the rate of final consumption so that sales promotion has tended to become concentrated at the retail level. Where trade promotion is intended to increase the number of retailers and wholesalers prepared to handle the product, the same result can be achieved more directly if a manufacturer can make his product so attractive to the customer that distributors cannot afford not to deal with it. However, in a static market with established brands, increases in sales can only be achieved by gaining market share at the expense of competitors. Heavy sales promotion by one company usually generates a similar response from its competitors. A dealer is more likely to switch brands permanently if the mark-up he receives increases, so raising his overall profitability. However, a higher mark-up means a higher price which can reduce demand or manufacturer profit margins.

8.5 Types of Sales Promotion

There are many types of sales promotion and the choice of which to use will be based on estimates of its likely effects. Sales promotion attempts to change buyer preferences when the purchase is made by providing something different and attractive. Some promotions are self-defeating since they produce temporary increases in sales as dealers and consumers stock up, but they are followed by a lull in the market while stocks gradually return to their pre-promotion level.

8.5.1 Branding

There is nothing new about branding. It was used by the craft guilds in the Middle Ages, and then, as now, its purpose was to indicate the identity of the maker and to be a guarantee of quality. With the arrival of many consumer goods, branding became more important as the need for it in terms of everyday identification increased. **Convenience goods** need to be distinguished by both the manufacturer and consumer because their functions, and in many cases qualities, are similar if not identical. Building up the brand image is necessary to create a group of loyal users. This is particularly important where the fixed costs of production are high and capacity needs to be fully used to take up economies of scale.

Brands are guarantees of quality and consistency. Poor quality control either during manufacture or in the distribution network can damage a brand irreparably. Sales of a well-managed brand increase because the risk of purchasing is reduced as customers feel secure about what they are buying. If people are satisfied, goodwill passes towards the brand and the product becomes less of a convenience good. Its demand is less elastic, which gives the manufacturer greater pricing freedom. Higher prices can go towards the cost of promotion and quality control. Larger dealer margins make the product more attractive to distributors, so giving it a stronger position when it comes to expanding the order size or the number of outlets used.

The choice of brand name is not easy. Ideally it should be short, distinctive and reflect the product characteristics and image. 'Babe' for a perfume, and 'Jaguar' for a car are examples of successful names because they conjure up desirable connotations and are suggestive of the features of the product. Some purchases are more overlaid with irrational and emotional factors than others and these products lend themselves to branding because of the opportunity to create an image which is distinctive. The image is an integral part of the purchase and the satisfaction obtained from the product. Branding is just one part of the whole package which goes to make up that image.

International markets present their own problems. Brand names do not always translate satisfactorily. Schwarzkopf, a German manufacturer of shampoos, when translated means 'blackhead'. Using the same name overseas can be unfortunate: Rolls-Royce had to rename its Silver Mist when it was exported to Germany, because 'mist' in German means 'dung'. In addition, names which are difficult to pronounce are unsatisfactory because people may fight shy of asking for the product. 'Noilly Prat', the original French vermouth, ran a series of advertisements explaining and underplaying the pronunciation.

Lastly, it is a legal requirement that the name has not already been taken by another company and registered.

The brand name which has all these characteristics is not easy to create. Computers are used to produce combinations of syllables to try to produce a name suitable for a new product. People work full time preparing new names for companies to use, and often a short list is tested by a panel of consumers. What companies are trying to do is find out what associations are conjured up by different names and the sound they make, but the results are dubious, almost any name producing a substantial percentage of replies linking it with washing powders, petrol, shampoo and some kind of packaged food. However, some form of testing is usually justified, and the wrong brand name can do irreparable damage to the product.

In deciding on a brand name the company can either choose a separate name for each product individually or use one name to cover a whole range as in 'Birds Eye' frozen foods. Each approach has its advantages and disadvantages. A name unique to one product means that it is not influenced by other products made by the company. If it fails it will not affect the sales of other products. Thus its progress can occur independently, and it can build up a unique personality. Using a brand name common to several products has the advantage that each can reinforce the other and the consumer is exposed to the brand name in many different areas. This reinforcement is desirable provided every item in the range meets up to the product image. Failure of a new product can adversely affect the rest, because the brand as a whole will get a bad name.

Many large distributors sell 'own brand' goods in addition to established brands. We all know of the different lines of instant coffee peculiar to distributors, e.g. Sainsbury's, Waitrose, etc. These are usually manufactured by the established brand companies, and are sold in competition with their brands. There are several reasons for this. It reflects the increased power of retailers and wholesalers, some of whom are large enough to carry their own brands. It can work to the manufacturer's advantage as well, since it guarantees a certain use of capacity and absolves the manufacturer from marketing costs associated with that sector of the market. It also allows greater flexibility in pricing and other promotion schemes, because these are now the province of the distributor. The established brand need not reduce its price and this allows it to perform in markets where price competition is not so great. A manufacturer entering a new market where there is considerable competition may not have the resources to undertake a costly promotion of a new brand. Selling direct to a distributor and taking his brand name enables the product to enter the market, on the strength of the distributor. In the case of own-brands, quality is just as important since poor product performance will lead to a loss of confidence in the retail outlet.

Not all products sell under brand names. Raw materials, fresh fruit and vegetables, for example, are often sold by product name. Industrial goods rarely need brands since the market is small and there is a close relationship between buyer and seller. However, at the consumer level the link between customer and manufacturer is much less direct, and often the technicalities of the product are beyond the average buyer. A brand name synonomous with quality allows a customer to buy a complex product such as an amplifier or automatic washing machine and feel confident about the expected performance.

8.5.2 Packaging
Packaging performs two functions. One is to protect the product and the other is to make it desirable and more attractive than its competitors.

The pack must be able to prevent damage to the product on its path through the distribution network and, in many cases, during its life with the final consumer. A pack of cornflakes has to prevent the cornflakes from being pulverised before they reach the customer, and needs to be sufficiently sealable to keep the cereal fresh and crisp once opened. When designing large bottles for fizzy drinks the fastener has to be capable of retaining the gas, hence the screw cap. Unexposed film and photographic paper have to be packed in opaque containers to prevent light from getting in – as do a number of anti-dandruff shampoos!

The way in which the pack is handled also influences its design. If wholesalers and retailers are heavily mechanised then the packaging must reflect this; for example, bulk packages which can be put on pallets and then shifted easily with fork lift trucks. As distribution chains become longer and storage requirements increase, the packaging should be designed to use the minimum of space. In this way a manufacturer may be able to steal a lead over competitors. All products are competing for space on retailers' shelves, and efficient use of space can often mean that more stock is actually on display.

Provided that the pack satisfies the protection criteria and the quality of the product is maintained, its outward appearance can have a significant impact on sales. With self-service outlets the principal way the product is brought to the attention of customers is through its packaging and it needs to be distinctive at a distance. In many cases the pack becomes more important to sales than the product itself. Products like butter, toothpaste, shaving foam and cigarettes all sell, in part, because of the way they are presented. Since the actual toothpaste or butter cannot be inspected, the choice of brand often depends on the image that the pack generates.

The design should be closely linked to the advertising so that it reminds consumers of the advertising message, and the appearance must fit with the product image. Inferior packaging may defeat the rest of the promotion if the product is presented as a quality item. Poor or unimaginative packaging can consign a product to oblivion.

In making final decisions about packaging, the methods used by competitors affect the choice. Tubes, cans, bottles and boxes all suit different products and market resistance to any one of them for a particular product is a limiting factor. Cost restricts choice. Expensive packaging of a cheap product is not only uneconomic, it is positively dangerous because it upsets people's perception of the value of the product, and introduces uncertainty and risk into the purchase. Similarly, too cheap a pack will prevent the product from appealing to the right sector of the market. For luxury goods, expensive packaging may be a strong selling point. 'After Eight' mints gain from individual wrapping because it gives the impression of luxury, wooden boxes for liqueur chocolates makes them more exclusive. Higher prices that more than cover the additional costs of expensive packaging may actually increase sales.

The size of the pack affects sales, and care must be taken to see that it suits market requirements. It may be cheaper to sell soup in two-litre cans but if that size is too large for most people's larders the cans will not sell. Sometimes large packets of products may carry too high a price, psychologically, for buyers to spend so much at one time. Size needs to be determined partly by the average household and their usage so that the product does not deteriorate while open at home. Just as satisfaction with a product reminds the customer to buy the same pack again, so disappointment as surely marks the pack as the one to avoid.

Shape and colour are significant factors in influencing purchases. When Mateus Rosé was introduced in an unusually shaped bottled it gained enormously from it. The difference in shape from a normal wine bottle separated it out and many people saw the bottle as having uses once the contents has been consumed – witness the number of bottle lamps. Packs that can be used in this way have the added advantage of providing a continuous reminder of the product. Many firms have at times used the pack as a special promotion and people may switch to the product to make use of this. Examples would include coffee sold in jars which can be used in the kitchen when empty, or mustard sold in tumblers, and so on. Successfully attracting new users who then remain buyers of the brand because they like the product represents a big return on packaging.

Just as the mass market for colour televisions has created a whole new side to advertising, so the colour of packs is able to increase the desirability of a product. We all have associations with colours: reds and oranges are warm, while blues and greens are colder and calmer; black carries connotations of power. The psychological impact of colour is so strong that it can alter people's opinions about a product. Blind tasting of wines and cigarettes often produce interesting results reflecting the importance of pack design and advertising.

8.5.3 Price Reductions

Price reductions can be effective ways of stimulating demand if the products are price elastic. However, special offers may build up resistance in customers who will only buy when an offer is available, and may increase their price awareness. Once the offer stops, the customer can become disgruntled and change to a competitor's product. At the same time, sales promotion works because it is 'special' and so requires frequent change, but this may cause confusion in the market. British Rail, in common with many other carriers, has been faced with this problem because of the range and complexity of fares that are available. If customers cannot understand when they are eligible for discounts, those discounts have no selling power. Offers may cheapen the image of the product and thus be counter-productive especially if advertising has been employed to build up an 'exclusive' product.

8.5.4 Credit Policy

As the standard of living has risen with increased wealth in the developed countries, there has been a shift to purchases of consumer durables such as cars and electrical goods. Unlike food and day-to-day expenses, the cost of consumer durables can represent several weeks' or months' wages. Financing their purchase requires careful budgeting. Inflation has made the problem more acute because people feel that by the time they have saved sufficient for a product its price will have risen again. A squeeze on incomes may cause people to delay purchases of consumer durables or to postpone replacement of existing equipment. To overcome this, and to enable expensive goods to be purchased before they can be paid for in full, many stores offer hire-purchase facilities where a deposit has to be put down at the time of purchase and the balance paid over a period of time. The effectiveness of this can be seen by the size of consumer credit – some £4,300m. in 1979 – and the effect on sales of a credit squeeze enforced by governments as part of their monetary control policies. If a store can offer good credit, customers will tend to buy there. Accounts and credit card facilities can determine which outlet is used. They have the advantage of enabling the customer to buy something without the feeling of having really paid for it. Credit is a convenience for the customer. It reduces the need to carry large quantities of cash. For example, someone who travels long distances can buy petrol when he needs it without having huge wads of pound notes. Although for some credit cards the retailer has to pay 5 per cent of the value of each sale, the provision of credit facilities may provide much more custom and so finance that loss. Of course, eventually the day of reckoning comes for the customer but the purchase has been made by then. The constraint on credit is its cost. A hire-purchase agreement allows the purchaser to pay over a period of time but the total paid is greater than the cash price, to cover the interest. Some stores offer their own extended free credit terms on purchases of sufficient value as an incentive to buy. In this case the store has to finance that credit because it represents money tied up which it cannot use. The opportunity cost of providing credit must not be greater than the returns on the faster turnover of stocks and larger clientele.

8.5.5 Other Forms of Sales Promotion

Assistance is often given to wholesalers and retailers in an attempt to encourage sales. Display materials are used both to attract attention in shop windows and to provide efficient storage inside. Rotating book stands, pack dispensers such as Tic Tac provide, bins filled with the product, are acceptable to the retailer if they help him to display his merchandise efficiently. Trade exhibitions allow the manufacturer to meet the trade and determine the likely response to its products. For the launch of a new product or the provision of information on the way a product works, exhibitions can be very useful. Some sales forces provide demonstrations of products in stores. This only makes sense where the market is well defined and the customers of the store are largely potential customers for the product, because it is very expensive in terms of personnel and sales space.

Free samples are effective but expensive. For a new product people have the opportunity to see what it is like before commiting themselves to purchase. If expectations are fulfilled this can be a persuasive way of creating sales. One manufacturer trying to establish his company in the market promoted a new brand of tea by offering a free tea bag. Demand for this promotion so far outstripped what had been anticipated that the firm had to devote a factory to producing more tea bags, and the cost of this exercise almost broke the company. Special introductory offers either in the store or from coupons mailed to customers' houses can encourage people to take a gamble if they are well presented.

Free gifts can persuade potential customers to buy products. Cereal manufacturers have used this in the past by putting a small toy in their packets and relying on children pressing their mothers to buy so that they can have the toy. These can pose problems of opened and broken packets at home where the toy has been removed but the product not consumed. As always, care must be taken in deciding how to go about promoting a product with a free gift, because it can influence the perceptions of the product. A soap powder manufacturer included a free duster with every pack of a new powder that was being launched. Sales were poor because customers thought that the company was doing them out of powder in the space taken up by the duster. Had they put the duster outside the pack, the promotion might have been very successful.

Many packs carry coupons to allow reductions on subsequent purchases of the product although the rate of redemption of these is not very high and dealers may accept them for other products. Competitions can encourage purchases and are more effective if they carry at least one high value prize. Asking entrants to complete a slogan may encourage them to think about the product as well as providing interest and demanding some skill. However, often they are won by a small group of almost professional competition entrants.

Trading stamps, self-liquidating offers where products are sold at a low price in return for a given number of packet tops, collecting items to make a set are all used to encourage purchases but they are increasingly under pressure from discount prices which seem to have stronger selling power.

8.6 Conclusion

Distributors and manufacturers view sales promotion in different ways. A special offer or display material is part of a concentrated effort by manufacturers to sell their products. However, space for display material is limited, and high cost promotions do not last long. For the distributor promotions are desirable if they attract more customers to the outlet. Once there, the distributor is not too concerned whether the products on offer are purchased. If the store is well laid out the customer may buy a wide range of goods. Thus a special promotion is seen as a way of increasing all sales rather than just those of the product.

Selling and sales promotion have important parts to play in influencing the purchasing decision. Because much of modern household buying is carried out in supermarkets where the product must sell itself, more attention is being shown to sales promotion. Research suggests that many people enter a shop with only a vague idea of what they want, and they can be persuaded to buy a whole range of goods they had not considered before seeing them as they walk through. Impulse buying is very important and special offers can be effective at encouraging this. Men and children are particularly susceptible to such tactics, particularly in buying small luxuries. Special offers at the checkouts are successful because they seem to have a cumulative impact as people queue for their turn at the till. Fully stocked shelves and huge stacked displays of cans or jars encourage sales as people seem mesmerised by the bounty of goodies. And lastly, a special offer gives the salesman something to talk about, so engaging the buyer's attention on a product for longer.

Work Section

A. Revision Questions

A1 How does selling differ from advertising?

A2 What are the functions of the sales force?

A3 List the seven factors that influence the sales quota set for each sales team.

A4 What methods are used to pay the sales force?

A5 Why is motivation and support so necessary for effective selling?

A6 What are the three ways that sales promotion can increase sales?

A7 List four types of sales promotion.

A8 Why is packaging so important?

A9 What are the key characteristics of a brand name?

A10 Why has sales promotion become increasingly important at the retail stage of the distribution channel?

A11 In what ways does the view of sales promotion differ between manufacturer and distributor?

A12 How can sales promotion be linked to the mix?

B. Exercises/Case Studies

B1 DLM Ltd manufactures five types of industrial equipment. Although the market for each type is different, the company has organised its sales force geographically, with teams selling the full range of machinery in five areas. The sales manager notes that each region has a different product as its best seller, but he does not believe that sales by type should vary significantly between regions because the industries using the machinery are evenly spread out. He is considering whether to reorganise the sales teams so that they each look after one product and cover the whole country. What are the advantages of each system and which would you advise the sales manager to choose?

B2 A company has developed a new toothpaste to add to its range of personal toiletries. It is a superior product to any other on the market, with better properties to fight tooth decay. A consumer panel has tested the toothpaste, and its flavour has been approved as well as its freshness. The price will be slightly above others on the market but this should not prove a problem once the toothpaste has become established, because of its better performance. Competitors are currently using various types of sales promotion on existing brands. What are the advantages and disadvantages to the firm of using promotion techniques, and what would you advise it to do in this case?

B3 Hamelin Brothers is a chain of stores selling musical instruments. It wants to increase sales because its stock levels are high. Economic forecasts indicate a forthcoming recession which is likely to hit its business. What kind of sales promotion might prove most helpful and why?

B4 When Cadburys launched 'Marvel' it was the only important brand in the dried milk market. There are two types of dried milk: one is dried skimmed milk and the other known as 'filled milk', a mixture of skimmed milk and vegetable fats. The latter tastes more like milk when added to water. At the time Marvel was launched it was thought that 'filled milks' could not be called milk products because of the vegetable fat additive, so Cadburys decided to market the skimmed milk product. The product was positioned as a substitute for milk with an attraction for slimmers as a secondary selling point.

By 1972 the market had levelled off, split roughly equally between 'own brands' and Marvel, at a total value of around £11m. Advertising of Marvel was steady at £½m. p.a. and began to move away from the fresh milk substitute to the slimmers' market with the emphasis on its contribution to calorie controlled diets.

Meanwhile St Ivel, with a good name for dairy products, had launched a filled milk called Miracle into the catering trade. It has rapidly become the brand leader.

In 1976 St Ivel decided to launch a filled milk into the consumer market. This product, called 'Five Pints', was packed in a plastic container shaped like a milk bottle. The product was aimed at the market as a stand-by for milk that was as good as milk. Sales were impressive and by the end of the year St Ivel had 20 per cent of the dried milk market, rising to 42 per cent in 1978. Cadbury responded to the challenge by marketing its own filled milk called 'Pint Size'. By 1978 the value of the total market had risen to £25m. from £11m. in 1972.

a. Why do you think St Ivel's 'Five Pints' was so successful? What forms of sales promotion worked in its favour?

b. Why did Cadbury not produce a filled milk earlier?

c. Account for the growth in the total market.

B5 In 1960 Smiths Potato Crisps Ltd held 80 per cent of the UK crisp market, and crisps accounted for 4/5ths of its total sales. However, in 1961 Imperial Tobacco bought a small crisps manufacturer in Scotland and began to sell crisps under the name 'Golden Wonder'. By 1966 Golden Wonder had gained 40 per cent of the £40m. UK crisp market. Sales in the crisp market had been rising at around 15 per cent p.a. Promotion and the introduction of a range of flavours were expected to continue this increase.

Production at Smiths was spread between fifteen different plants throughout the country. Seven of these had been modernised and their products compared well with competitors' crisps. The remainder were inefficient and the product inferior. Production was spread out in fifteen different plants because of the poor keeping qualities of crisps. In the existing packaging they had a life of three or four days before they lost some of their crispness and flavour. Consequently, at the retail end of the market, stocks were small and display minimal. Neither manufacturer nor distributor could prepare for seasonal increases in demand by building up stocks.

Smiths packed crisps in four sizes, from 1 oz to 7 oz, ranging from 2p to 12½p.[1] In 1964 Smiths introduced a new film packaging which extended the shelf life of the product to two weeks and was visually effective. This packaging was used for the large sizes, but because of the higher cost of the film the 2p size was still packed in the old material. In 1965 Golden Wonder launched a 2p size packed in film and distributed it nationally. The Golden Wonder product was advertised and backed by a promotion scheme for the trade. Retailers were encouraged to display the product. As a result, because the Smiths equivalent deteriorated faster, retailers could not display it and dissatisfaction with the product caused some outlets to drop the brand. Smiths reacted by introducing the new packaging for the 2p size, but it expected to remove most of the profit margin as a result.

Smiths sales force consisted of nine area managers who were in charge of forty sales representatives and 120 van salesmen. The area managers spent some time dealing with wholesalers and major retail accounts. The sales representatives visited outlets, checking the freshness of stock and dealing with any queries or complaints. They covered their area in eight-week cycles. Van salesman delivered once a week or once a fortnight depending on the size of the order. Twenty per cent of orders were handled by van salesman and the rest ordered direct (if they ordered more than ten cases per week) or bought through wholesalers. Golden Wonder, in contrast, employed few van salesman and concentrated its selling effort on large retail outlets and wholesalers, ignoring orders of less than ten cases per week. Wholesalers preferred Golden Wonder products although the mark up was only slightly better than Smiths (16⅔ per cent against 16¼). However, Golden Wonder used several promotion campaigns to maintain wholesaler interest.

a. What is the importance of packaging for the crisp market?
b. How would you have altered Smiths sales policy to increase its market share?

---

[1] Decimal equivalents have been used in this case.

C. Essay Questions

C1 How important is sales policy and how can it be fitted into the mix?

C2 Explain the role of the sales force and suggest how it might be organised.

C3 How can branding a product help sales?

C4 What is the difference between advertising and sales policy?

C5 'All forms of sales promotion are likely to increase sales, so companies should always include some incentives in their sales policy.' Discuss.

Chapter 9

Pricing

Objective: *To explain the meaning of price and its impact on the market. To examine the various methods for setting prices and the constraints that exist, limiting firm's action. To suggest a basis for pricing strategy.*

Synopsis: *Price plays a vital role in determining the firm's profitability. It needs to be set within the constraints of the market place and Government intervention. There are five common methods of pricing which are limited by the objectives of the company and the way consumers view the price relative to the product.*

Plan of the chapter:

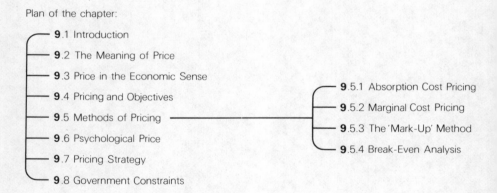

- **9**.1 Introduction
- **9**.2 The Meaning of Price
- **9**.3 Price in the Economic Sense
- **9**.4 Pricing and Objectives
- **9**.5 Methods of Pricing
  - **9**.5.1 Absorption Cost Pricing
  - **9**.5.2 Marginal Cost Pricing
  - **9**.5.3 The 'Mark-Up' Method
  - **9**.5.4 Break-Even Analysis
- **9**.6 Psychological Price
- **9**.7 Pricing Strategy
- **9**.8 Government Constraints

9.1 Introduction

The price of a product is a fundamental part of the whole marketing mix since it is the one, immediate comparison that can be made between products. We use it in a broad way to judge products: this can of beans costs more than that one; either we buy a new jacket or a radio for the car, and so on. Yet price is only part of the mix and by no means the only factor that affects our choice. The image of the product, what we want it to say about ourselves, the ease with which we can purchase it, the after-sales service we can expect, all contribute to the decision in many ways. However, it is much more difficult to compare these factors in an objective way, while price at least gives the illusion of objectivity. It is, after all, measured in a unit which is common to almost all products – money. Of course, there are products which cannot easily be priced. A painting may be considered priceless, and there is something uncomfortable about insurance companies which put a price on limbs or life. Nevertheless, price plays an important part in the capitalist system and this chapter sets out to explain the factors that influence price and how firms come to put a price on their products.

9.2 The Meaning of Price

At first sight, the price of a product is clear. Instant coffee is priced around £2 for a 200 g jar, an amplifier is priced at £100 and so on. Yet in practice, price is much more difficult to define. It means very different things to different people. A retailer will look at the price of a product as being the 'total price' he has to pay. This will include what he pays the manufacturer or wholesaler, any discounts or offers he makes, plus some estimate of the cost of after-sales service, the shelf space the product uses, storage, and how well it fits into the overall range of goods. he sells. While he may not quantify all these factors, he will have some idea, however intuitive, of the profit he may expect. In deciding whether to stock the product he will compare the 'total price' with that of other manufacturers.

Even at the final consumer level, the price of a product may not be all that clear. Recently there has been a considerable growth in 'pick-your-own' fruit which is usually 'cheaper' than fruit bought at a shop. On price alone, strawberries which cost 50p per pound are more expensive than a similar pound at 40p. However, in the first case the fruit is ready packed at the shop, while in the second the customer has to go to a 'pick-your-own' farm and spend time gathering it. Which is now the cheaper? The answer depends on the value you put on your labour, the 'freshness' of fruit you want, the enjoyment you get from doing your own picking. Comparisons in price can really only be satisfactorily made when you know exactly what you are buying. Purchasing hi-fi equipment at a discount store where there are no after-sales facilities may only be cheaper than buying from an ordinary retailer until something goes wrong.

9.3 Price in the Economic Sense

Economists have built up a large body of price theory. For the economy as a whole, the price of a product influences the payments made to the **factors of production** (land, labour, capital, managerial ability) that went into its manufacture. This includes the level of profit, which may influence the decision of a firm to enter or leave the industry. In this way the demand for labour, investment and land will alter in response to the expected return on capital, and the geographical distribution of industry may change. It would be wrong to assume that price and profit were the only factors in the decision, but they do play an important part. The **price system** is an inefficient means of allocating factors of production because labour and capital are not particularly mobile and the response to high profits may take many years to work through. In the case of a highly efficient industry yielding good returns, others who wish to join it may be prevented by barriers to entry. These can take several forms. If there is a strong brand loyalty the cost of advertising and promotion necessary to break into the market could be prohibitive. High fixed overheads in production and distribution mean that sales volume must be large to achieve reasonable economies of scale and this may not be feasible for a new company. Equally, technical knowledge built up over a long period will give existing firms a strong advantage. In addition, a company wishing to shift to a more profitable industry may be faced with problems in running down existing inefficient industries – problems increased by Government intervention to maintain and assist those industries – especially in areas of high unemployment. The greater the investment in an industry, the less flexible it is, since firms need to obtain a reasonable return on their capital and hence maintain production, provided it is yielding a sufficient minimum profit.

We saw in Chapter 3 that one of the principal determinants of demand was price, and that for most goods there was some relationship between the amount demanded and the price of the product. The same is true in a limited way for supply. As price increases, it is likely that more of a product will be offered for sale because the returns from each sale are rising. If profits rise then other producers may be attracted into the industry, so increasing supply. Economists believe that there is some equilibrium price and quantity where the amount supplied and demanded are the same. Figure 9.1 shows this relationship with an equilibrium price p_0 and quantity demanded and supplied q_0.

In the stock market the price of a share is determined by the number for

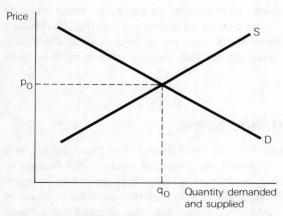

Fig. 9.1 Equilibrium price in a free market

sale and the demand for them. Similarly at an auction, or even at a vegetable market, where towards the end of the day prices fall to get rid of any stock that is still unsold. Intense competition by airlines has meant that price has affected both the decision over which airline to travel by, and also the number of seats available. When Freddie Laker introduced the cut-price Skytrain to America, the major transatlantic carriers rapidly responded by introducing their own form of cheap travel on scheduled services. However, for most markets, the problems are far greater since supply is not very flexible and cannot be rapidly altered to suit changes in market conditions. To increase output may involve expanding the size of the plant which requires expenditure on new investment, or the change in demand may be short lived and the company may not consider it worthwile altering output. In such cases, if the demand for a product varies significantly from the supply at the going price, a 'black market' may develop. Then, because of a shortfall of supply, those consumers who can obtain the product may resell it at a higher price. Recently, British Leyland has been plagued with such problems over Land-Rovers and Range-Rovers. In the case of a surplus, retailers will find that they cannot move their stock quickly enough and in addition to reducing future orders for the product, they may cut back on all the products manufactured by the same firm. From this, we can see that the manufacturer needs to keep some idea of what the market for his product is, so that he can avoid serious shortages or surpluses. Both create dissatisfaction from consumers and retailers.

9.4 Pricing and Objectives

The pricing decision is dependent on the objectives of the firm. Price is important in determining sales volume and profits. Some firms put profit maximisation as their key objective and their pricing policies will differ from those of firms with growth as a major objective.

Price is not the only factor that affects demand, and its importance varies with the state of the economy. When the economy is healthy, incomes are growing and the standard of living is high, price plays a less important role in determining demand. If the economy is contracting, price becomes more significant in the purchase decision. Nevertheless, price does have an impact on market share and the position of a company with respect to its competitors, and increasingly firms have had to take this into consideration. When price is determined on the basis of costs alone, profit margins are related to total profit objectives, and the resulting price is compared to those charged by competitors. Alternatively firms may examine the market and take the competitive price for a product as the basis for their own price. They then decide on levels of production to give the desired contribution. If the firm cannot produce at the necessary cost level then the product will not be manufactured. The problem with this approach is that it assumes the competitors have priced their products correctly.

A firm might have growth as its prime objective. In this case, one course of action would be to try to undercut competitors. This method is often used by late entrants to an established market, or by small firms trying to obtain a share of the market. The small firm may have low overheads and be able to achieve a reasonable profit with low prices, but if demand for the product is strong the firm may be forced to expand, so losing its cost advantage. Eventually prices may have to rise, removing the competitive edge.

Prices are also cut by large firms trying to protect their markets from competition, or set deliberately low when introducing a new product to discourage others from entering the market. Problems can emerge if the low price does not succeed in preventing competition since the volume each firm can sell may fall with an increase in the number of producers.

Using price as a means of achieving a given market share or preventing competition is a frequent technique employed in markets where there is one company with a significantly larger proportion of the market than any of its competitors. The company is usually the price leader. Its prices form the yardstick by which others set their prices, and a shift in price by this company will usually have repercussions throughout the industry. How quickly other firms respond depends on the direction of a price change. If prices are raised, competitors may wait to see the effect on the market before changing theirs. In a competitive market a reduction in price by the price leader is likely to be followed swiftly by others in the industry.

Firms that are not market leaders often determine their prices by placing them at or near the 'prevailing price'. This is particularly true of industries where there is little difference between individual firm's products, and where there is a general awareness of the market price. In this situation there is little to be gained by differing sharply from the established price since undercutting may lead to a loss of profit because of increased costs incurred by higher production levels. However, exceeding the market price may well lead to a sharp fall in the quantities sold, especially if competitors' products are easily available. If there is a distinctive characteristic of the product, the price may be set above the market price, appealing to quality and status.

In industries where there are few firms selling very similar products, one of the major pricing objectives may be that of stability. Tacit agreement between the companies on the basic price of the product ensures that price-cutting wars do not take place. This is not necessarily something that hurts the consumer. Price instability leads to confusion in markets and may reduce the service offered to the consumer in the long run. For this reason the price of petrol, for example, is set at much the same level by all the major oil companies. Occasionally price wars do break out, but the oil companies try to avoid this because, finally, each company finds itself making less profit, and to compensate for this low volume petrol stations may close.

Nationalised industries are a special category. Since they are not accountable to shareholders the need for profit maximising or profit satisficing is not present. They are involved in providing a service or product for the benefit of the country as a whole. In the case of a service such as the railways, profit is not feasible – no railway in Europe makes a profit, but governments have felt that the service is essential. While different governments provide different criteria against which the performance of the nationalised industries is judged, they are expected to operate according to 'commercial principles'. The problem is that these commercial principles are not defined. In the last thirty years both marginal cost pricing and full cost pricing have been used in different industries (See section 9.5). Broadly, the nationalised industries are expected to set the lowest price consistent with covering costs. However, their flexibility in pricing has been severely curtailed by price controls which have been applied for extended periods in recent years.

9.5 Methods of Pricing

Many firms use a 'cost plus' approach to pricing. Taken at its simplest, this means that firms calculate the cost of producing a product and then add on a profit margin. These methods imply that price is not an important determinant of demand, for they make no concessions to the market. They assume that the product will sell at the price in question. The other extreme is to raise the price until sales fall back seriously. The costs of manufacture are largely ignored. The main constraints on the price depend on the strength of demand for the product and its price elasticity, the level of competition and the closeness of substitutes, and lastly the psychological factors of price that affect demand.

It is true, in general terms, that no firm can afford to sell all its products below cost, but most cost methods of pricing ignore the market in that there is no attempt to equate what consumers are prepared to pay for a product with the price that will give the firm a reasonable return on its investment. The major problems only become apparent when what consumers are prepared to pay is far removed from the price firms charge, and usually notice is only taken when products are overpriced and do not sell.

9.5.1 Absorption (or Full Cost) Cost Pricing
The principle of this pricing method is to reduce total costs to unit costs. This reflects accounting convention that **costs** can be split into **direct costs** and overheads. Direct costs such as raw materials, and in some cases labour (e.g. part-time employment and overtime), can be allocated to each unit produced. Some of these costs are dependent on volume through discounts on bulk purchases of raw materials. However, overheads cannot be allocated so easily. The administrative and selling overheads exist regardless of output, although they may expand as the organisation does. Similarly, machinery incurs fixed costs which need to be distributed over the range of products. Inevitably the allocation tends to be arbitrary, based for example on a percentage of all sales, or area of factory space used by the manufacture of each product. Once this

allocation is made, an estimate of sales volume is drawn up and the overheads are broken down to give a cost per unit. To the sum of direct costs and allocated overhead is added some percentage margin to cover profit.

Consider the following example:

Michael and David Ridley are directors of Ridley Brothers, a small firm making electrical switches for a specialist lamp manufacturer. They make three types of switch – the A/100, A/110 and A/130. They are pricing their products and they feel that the matter can be decided by referring to the cost of production. In previous years figures show that the firm has made a profit of 10 per cent on each switch sold. The cost information is set out below:

Switch type	A/100	A/110	A/130
Labour per unit	5p	7p	10p
Material per unit	3p	6p	10p

In addition there are overheads of sales and administration of £1,000 and cost of capital £500.

At first the directors are uncertain what to do about the overheads. They consider allocating them equally between the switches but finally decide that a more reasonable approach would be to split the £1,500 according to sales levels. Consequently they estimate sales that they should receive, based on an initial experimental order from the lamp manufacturer:

Switch type	A/100	A/110	A/130
Sales (no. of switches)	1,000	700	300
Per cent of total	50%	35%	15%
Overheads	£750	£525	£225
O/h per unit	75p	75p	75p

Armed with this, they calculate the cost of manufacturing each switch and add in a 10 per cent profit margin:

Total cost/unit	83p	88p	95p
10% profit	8.3p(8p)	8.8p(9p)	9.5p(10p)
Final price	91p	97p	£1.05

This gave them a total revenue of £1,904 and total cost of £1,731, leaving a profit of £173. Satisfied with this, production went ahead and once the first 100 A/100 switches were delivered Michael noted that they had made a profit of 100 × 8p = £8. However, David pointed out that he had just paid £100 in secretarial wages. Something did not seem right.

In addition to ignoring the price that the market would be prepared to pay, the method assumes that all output will be sold. A lower sales volume puts up the unit cost since overheads now have to be spread over a smaller number of units sold. However, this is not reflected in the price so the profit margin of 10 per cent is not reached. Pricing in this way also implies that a profit can be made from the first unit sold. This is demonstrably not so, since there are overheads of £1,500 which will be incurred regardless of the number of switches sold.

9.5.2 Marginal Cost Pricing

The marginal cost of production is the addition to total costs incurred by producing one more unit of output. To calculate the marginal cost, the firm needs to distinguish between those costs which vary with output and are directly attributable to each unit produced, and those costs which remain fixed regardless of output. A price is set for the product and the direct costs are subtracted from that price. The balance represents a contribution to the overheads. This underlines the point that each unit does not make a profit, and it allows an examination of profitability as sales increase or decrease.

The Ridley brothers were unhappy about their system for determining price, and they decided to look at alternative methods. David then suggested the marginal cost approach and they considered this carefully. They decided on three prices: 90p, £1.00 and £1.10. (Overheads are £1,500)

Switch type	A/100	A/110	A/130
Direct costs (unit)	8p	13p	20p
Price	90p	£1.00	£1.10
Contribution (unit)	82p	87p	90p
Sales	1,000	700	300
Contribution	£820	£609	£270

$$\therefore \textit{ Total contribution } = £1,699$$
to overheads of £1,500

= Profit of £199

Michael and David agreed that this method allowed them to see the relative strength of each line and did not imply an immediate profit on each sale. At the same time, David saw that with the possible doubling of the order for the A/100 they could immediately calculate the effects on profitability without having to redistribute overheads in line with the changed sales pattern. If sales of the A/100 rose by 1,000 units then the new contribution would be 2 × £820 = £1,640 and the new total profit would rise by £820 to £1,019.

The marginal cost approach has the advantage that it enables firms to set prices purely on direct costs when sales are sluggish. For example, the tourist trade is seasonal and this means that in off-peak times use of hotels and airlines is low. However, the fixed costs remain the same. The hotel still has as many rooms, and the airline cannot reduce the size of its fleet. In addition costs associated with both enterprises in the form of administration and management expertise continue. An airline cannot lay off its pilots during the winter just because the demand for their services is slack. So in these periods airlines and hotels try to keep usage up by reducing prices and offering special deals to 'off-peak' travellers. Assuming that peak-season rates provide sufficient contribution to cover overheads, any positive contribution in the off-peak times adds to profit.

Marginal cost pricing is frequently used by firms which are not operating at full capacity. Many large retailers carry 'own-brand' products made by established manufacturers. These usually sell at lower prices than the established brand but they relieve the manufacturer of selling and distribution expenses. Provided that the sale of 'own-brand' lines does not seriously reduce the sales of established brands the manufacturer's profit will rise. In calculating the effect on profits, it is important to determine the extent of sales lost to 'own-brand' purchases against the contribution of the 'own-brand' sales.

Retailers also apply the marginal cost method in setting prices for selected products which act as 'loss leaders' to attract customers into shops. While these products may provide no contribution to overheads, retailers hope that once customers are in the shop they will make purchases of other goods which do provide a positive contribution. Again, this only raises total profits if new customers are attracted, or existing customers choose to purchase more goods than before.

As with absorption costing, little attempt to determine the strength of demand is made, apart from the estimate of total sales. In addition, it assumes a clear definition of costs and many types of cost do not fit as easily as the method suggests. In the case of marginal costing, it is often difficult to calculate the cost of making one more unit of output. Just how much labour is a direct cost and how much a fixed cost in the short term? Overtime, for example, can sometimes be cut or increased without much difficulty, directly dependent on the demand for the final product. In other cases it is a means of payment, standardised in all but name, to raise the take-home pay of em ployees.

Although marginal costing does have clear advantages over full costing, it has its pitfalls as well. A low priced product which makes little contribution while other strong products are providing sufficient contribution to cover overheads, may become so successful that increased fixed costs are called for, through expansion of manufacturing capacity or product supervision. Alternatively the strong products which are effectively carrying the low priced one may cease performing so well and consequently fail to cover the overheads. In this case the low priced product will have to contribute more to cover overheads, and its price will be increased, perhaps with a resultant fall in sales.

9.5.3 The 'Mark-Up' Method

Many retailers apply a standard mark-up on wholesale prices to give them their profit. Manufacturers are aware of this when setting prices but they have little control over the size of the mark-up. The 'recommended retail price' has had little meaning since the abolition of **Resale Price Maintenance** in most areas. (This control of the final price has almost totally disappeared. Books are one of the few remaining areas where control is exercised over the final price.) The only way in which manufacturers can control price is by limited franchising of retail outlets for their products. While the mark-up method of pricing may appear as merely an extension of full cost pricing, it is different because of its outlook, and the forces acting on it.

Unlike full cost pricing, which is production orientated and ignores the market situation, mark-up pricing takes the state of demand into consideration. If the products are not selling, the retailer will reduce the price to get his stock moving. If he is dissatisfied with the new mark-up, and demand does not pick up sufficiently for him to raise prices again, then he will not re-order from his suppliers. In this way, through pricing, the retailer may help a brand to establish itself, or cease stocking it completely. Retailers do not apply the same mark-up to all types of merchandise. Fresh foods may have a substantially lower mark-up than frozen or canned food. Luxury items may have a still larger mark-up. In each case the mark-up is calculated as a percentage of the wholesale price but its variations will reflect in part the level of competition. Retailers' prices for the same product in the same area, the age of the product and its brand strength all influence the size of the mark-up.

9.5.4 Break-Even Analysis

Another broad approach to pricing is through break-even analysis. This takes into consideration the market forces operating on the product as well as the costs of production. A price for the product is chosen and from this the total revenue curve can be constructed showing the increase in revenue resulting from increased sales. When compared with costs, the volume of output at which total costs equal total revenue can be shown. Above this break-even output, a profit is made on each unit and as output increases so will total and unit profit. Figure 9.2 (a) shows a simple break-even chart with one price level. It assumes that costs and price remain static, and that the types of cost are distinguishable.

In Fig. 9.2(b) three different prices are taken for the product. The price yielding TR_1 is higher than TR_2 and TR_3. As price is raised, so the break-even output falls and the profit on output above the break even rises more rapidly.

So far we have assumed that the firm can sell as much as it wants at the given price. If this were so, theoretically the firm could charge as much as it liked, but we know that this is not the case. In Chapter 3 we looked at the demand curve and saw that, for most products, more was demanded only as price fell. From this we can generate a total revenue curve based on the

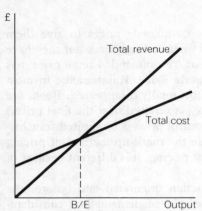

Fig. 9.2(a): A break-even chart

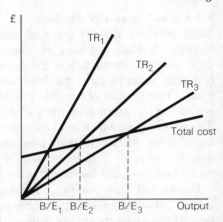

Fig. 9.2(b): A break-even chart

demand curve. While price elasticity is greater than one, reducing the price
will lead to an increase in total revenue. When the elasticity falls below one,
the percentage drop in price is greater than the percentage increase in quantity
demanded, and total revenue begins to fall because the increase in sales is only
brought about by a larger fall in the unit price. By combining the total revenue
curve from the demand curve with the break-even chart, it is possible to find
the output level and price which yields the greatest profit.

In Fig. 9.3 the price which gives TR₁ yields the highest profit since at that
revenue the vertical distance between a and the total cost line is greatest. The
total revenue derived from the demand curve is the boundary of possible sales
volume and price. This method of pricing is valuable for firms that face
reasonably steady costs, but of less use for enterprises whose costs fluctuate
widely and frequently, or at times of rapid inflation.

Break-even pricing enables the firm to link price, cost and volume of sales.
Having decided on the profit required, the firm can determine its price and
output.

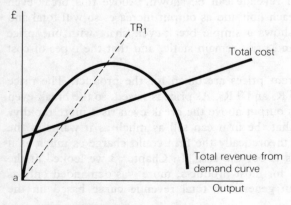

Fig. 9.3: Profit maximisation

9.6 Psychological Price

Increasingly, when products are being tested in the market to determine their 'fit' with consumer needs, price is a factor that is researched. People often have a clear idea of the value of a product. When similar products are already on the market, competitors' prices obviously affect this perceived value, but the consumer is constantly facing new products with new uses. Consumers quickly put their own value on these new products, and it is important for the manufacturer to price at a level which allows 'value for money'. Frequently, manufacturers set up user panels to evaluate the product and suggest a range of prices at which they would be prepared to buy the product. This gives the manufacturer some idea of acceptable prices, although what consumers say they will pay for a product and what, in practice, they do pay are sometimes different. However, this price range does give an indication of what the market is likely to bear. If the price is too low to give a reasonable return on investment then the firm will decide not to go ahead with the product. Often, however, research shows an acceptable price higher than the 'cost plus' or 'marginal cost' price. Sometimes this results in the manufacturer setting the price below perceived value in an attempt to raise sales. Such a move can be self-defeating since customers may view a product priced substantially below its perceived value with suspicion, wondering what is wrong with it. Similarly, if the price is well above the perceived value, they may ask what is so special about it. Figure 9.4 shows the information the customer needs, to justify a price outside the 'acceptable' range.

Price itself tells us about the product and is often used as an indication of quality. When the price is too high or too low the firm has to provide more information to explain the reasons and this puts up the marketing costs.

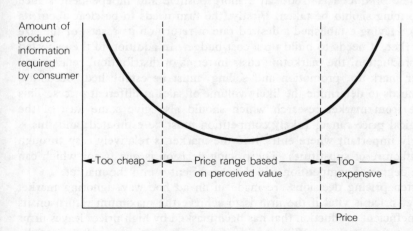

Fig. 9.4: The relationship between price and the information required to justify it.
(Adapted from *Directing the Marketing Effort* by R.L. Willsmer, p. 162, Pan)

We have already noted that price is only one of the factors that affects the purchasing decision, but it is important that it reflects the image of the product in terms of the way it is presented. The type of retail outlet and packaging affect people's perception of the product and its quality. If the packaging suggests an expensive product, but the price is cheap, potential customers may be deterred. In such a situation, firms may find that sales increase when price is increased. This complicates the elasticity relationships discussed in Chapter 3, but it emphasises the need to consider the product as a whole, rather than only in its constituent parts. All the factors need to be right before the customer buys without feeling he is taking some sort of risk.

Firms do not want to change prices frequently as this destabilises the market. However, it is easier to reduce price than increase it, and this suggests that it is safer to err on the side of a high price rather than set it too low and subsequently have to increase it. Once a price has been established a degree of flexibility can be introduced through special offers and discounts. This has the advantage of maintaining the correct perceived value price, while also appealing to people's wish for a bargain. It can be an effective way of increasing market share without creating a conflict between the product and how it is viewed. There are also certain price barriers. For example, a product priced at £9.99 may sell because it is 'under £10'!

9.7 Pricing Strategy

Many firms allow their prices to be set by the prevailing competition. While this may be satisfactory for a firm with a small share of an established market, when a new product is introduced a more positive and independent stance towards pricing should be taken. Firstly, the firm needs to be clear about its objectives. Having established a desired rate of return on its assets, or the size of the market, it needs to build up a cost budget. In addition to the expected costs of production, the marketing costs in terms of distribution, retailer and wholesaler mark-up, promotion and selling, must be established. Secondly, the firm needs to determine the likely volume of sales at different prices. This can come from market research which should also give some idea of the psychological price range. Likely competition must be estimated, and this is particularly important where entry into the market is relatively easy through the manufacture of substitutes. The pricing decision is one factor which can affect the degree of competition and the ease of entry into the market.

Too often pricing decisions are made in an ad hoc way, ignoring market forces. Yet price is vital if the firm is to achieve the maximum return on its capital. Inefficient production that has been masked by high prices leaves firms vulnerable to competition. With the increase in international trade, especially in finished goods, many British firms have been caught unawares.

9.8 Government Constraints

The freedom of the firm in setting its prices is limited by the Government. The Government has set up certain agencies which are involved in monitoring prices and profitability. Where a firm has more than 25 per cent of the market share it is liable to investigation by the Monopolies Commission. Excess profits are penalised by orders from the Commission to reduce prices or alter marketing strategies which are felt to be against the national interest. In addition, Britain has undergone a series of Prices and Incomes Policies which have limited the ability of firms to raise their prices. Various agencies such as the Price Commission have exercised control on prices, their judgements usually based on acceptable profit margins and allowable cost increases (e.g. raw materials). While these may be in the interest of the consumer, there is evidence that restriction of prices may have distorted the pattern of production and reduced the investment within an industry. Many firms complain that control of profits removes the incentive to increase efficiency.

Taxation has a direct influence on prices. Changes in indirect tax, such as VAT or excise duty, alter the price that the consumer has to pay without changing the revenue the company receives on each unit sold. However, an increase in the indirect tax can radically change demand, and so influence profits. In some cases firms try to absorb some of the increase so that sales volume is kept up, but the revenue they receive falls and reduces the total profit. Direct taxes, e.g. income tax, can reduce sales by reducing the income received by consumers. The extent of the effect on sales is dependent on the price elasticity of demand in the case of indirect taxation, and the income elasticity of demand for direct taxes.

Work Section

A. Revision Questions

A1 How can price allocate factors of production?

A2 What is a black market?

A3 What problems are there when comparing products by their price?

A4 When does price have least effect on demand?

A5 How do the firm's objectives influence its pricing policy?

A6 What is the basis of absorption cost pricing?

A7 List the advantages of marginal cost pricing.

A8 How does the 'mark-up' method differ in approach from absorption and marginal cost pricing?

A9 What is meant by psychological price?

A10 In what way can the Government influence pricing policies?

B. Exercises/Case Studies

B1 A company is manufacturing a product, using only half its capacity. The total overheads are allocated to its actual output and sales of 5,000 units. Direct costs are £5 per unit and overheads work out at £2 per unit. The product sells for £6.50. The company then receives an additional special order for 3,000 items which will be sold under the distributor's 'own-brand'. The price offered to the firm by the distributor is £6 per unit. Should the company take on this additional order? What factors other than price will influence its decision?

B2 Hillside Enterprises manufactures furniture. Currently, high stock levels are causing concern because of the money that is tied up. At the same time, the company is considering a new design for a chair. The market price is tentatively set at £25 and market research suggests a sales volume of 2,000 chairs in the first year, with a minimum of 1,500. If the design is successful sales could rise to 3,000 chairs. The distribution mark-up is 50 per cent. Fixed overheads will be £7,000 p.a. and direct costs are £8.50 per chair.

   a. What is the break-even output?

   b. Hillside Enterprises is considering making 1,800 chairs to begin with and it will only increase production if sales in the first six months are high. What profit will it make on the initial production run?

   c. If Hillside Enterprises want a profit of £3,000, how many chairs should it make?

d. If the company reduces the price to £22, sales are likely to be 3,500. Is this a sensible move in terms of profit? Show your working.

B3 Brecon Ltd was a manufacturer of fabric. The company produced a special cloth known as Item 100 as part of its competitive product lines. It was special, for a number of reasons. It was of good quality; it was produced in a department which could not be used for any other work; it was sold by trained salesmen who were paid on a straight salary. The central problem facing Brecon Ltd related to the price that it had to charge for Item 100. For some time the firm had been a price leader in the market but in recent years it was beginning to lose its grip as it was undercut by competitors who worked on a slender margin, but with little financial support and relatively high costs. Competitors charged 75p per yard while Brecon Ltd charged £1.00 per yard. The sales forecast for the whole industry was 800,000 yards in the coming year. The sales manager of Brecon believed that the firm could obtain a 25 per cent share of this market if the firm's price was reduced to 75p per yard. This he believed had two advantages; it would allow Brecon to reach new production levels and so avail itself of important economies of scale in labour and material costs; it would squeeze competitors hard and so stop any further price competition. If the price could not be reduced then Brecon believed it could sell 75,000 units at a minimum and 100,000 units at a maximum, with the price at £1.00.

Cost schedules for Brecon Ltd are set out in the following table:

Estimated cost in pence per yard of Item 100

Output	75,000 units	100,000 units	200,000units
Direct labour	28	26	16
Materials	17	17	14
Supervision and maintenance	16	15	18
Material spoilage	5	6	8

General overheads and selling costs had to be added on at 50 per cent of factory costs.

Taking into consideration the numerate and non-numerate information available, would you advise that the price be lowered to 75p or kept at £1.00? State your assumptions and reasoning.

B4 The Granham Company was an engineering firm, the main product of which was a pneumatic drill (designed basically for road construction). It was the largest supplier in the market where, at a standard price of £800, there was very little competition. With the home market reaching saturation point Granham began to look around for other markets to ensure it was kept up to full capacity.

It was at this point that the managing director received an offer for an order of 200 drills from a German construction firm, if the drills could be delivered to its factory, all expenses paid, at a price of £640 each. The immediate reaction was to jump at this offer as it would provide entry into a new market and, in the short term, production resources could always be redirected if necessary. Present cost structures suggested the opportunity ought to be seized:

	£
Direct labour	150
Materials	175
Variable overheads	90
Fixed overheads	120
Standard cost per unit	£535

However, to this cost structure had to be added freight charges and import duties and a sum of £30,000 was thought to be ample to cover this.

A quick decision was necessary, but aware of the fact that cost structures could easily have changed since the standard cost was set, it was necessary to ask the cost accountant for any additional information that could be provided on the product. He sent through the following information:

a. that labour wage rates and material purchase prices had a variance of 5 per cent above the standard shown;

b. there was to be an increase in internal overheads per unit of £30, part for administration and part (£24) as a result of the increase in fixed costs following the recent machine installation to provide for expansion.

Examine carefully the information available. Would you accept the new order bearing in mind:

● the numerate information available at the time the first offer arrived?

● the additional numerate information that the cost accountant provided?

● factors that have to be taken into consideration outside the numerate data available?

C. Essay Questions

C1 How would you develop a pricing strategy for a new product?

C2 Compare and contrast absorption and marginal cost pricing, evaluating the advantages of each method.

C3 What is marginal cost pricing? How might it be used (a) in the short term; (b) in the long term?

C4 How far can theoretical models be useful in explaining a firm's pricing policies? (Cambridge Local Examinations Syndicate 1977.2.5.)

C5 'Free competition is desirable because it is in the consumers' interests and ensures that industry is efficient'. Discuss.

C6 Should firms base their prices on costs if they are to make a profit?

C7 Is it always sensible to set prices as low as possible so that firms can take advantage of economies of scale?

C8 What factors should the firm consider when formulating its pricing policy as part of the mix?

C9 What differences, if any, are there in the principles involved in setting prices in public as compared with private enterprise?
(Cambridge Local Examinations Syndicate 1973.2.7.)

Chapter 10

Control and Review

Objective: *To show the necessity of control and review in marketing, and the way control information can be used to aid the firm in maintaining market share and market performance.*

Synopsis: *Control and review provide essential information on how products are selling, compared to the objectives that have been set. Marketing budgets present special problems because the relationship between expenditure, planned performance and results is both uncertain and constantly changing. However, analysis of performance enables the firm to modify its acitons in the light of new conditions. In this way opportunities for new products and markets can be seized as they occur, and the mix can be modified to give the best support for existing products. Careful use of budget and control information highlights problems as they occur. Refining the analysis can show the root cause of the problem so making efficient use of management time.*

Plan of the chapter:

10.1 Introduction

Enterprises make profits by generating more revenue than the costs they incur. Control and review are the means of ensuring that costs and returns are in line with the objectives and strategy of the company. Control information is a measure of how well products have done, the performance of each aspect of the mix and the actual size of departmental expenses. Review analyses the information against the budget figures. This allows the company to change its decisions in the light of new evidence about the market place. There should be frequent reports on the progress of each product so that any divergence between what is actually happening and the plan can be analysed. In this way problems are highlighted and can be dealt with quickly before too much damage is caused. Because conditions and relationships often change, budgets have to be modified, but this does not mean that budgets have no useful part to play. It is easy to let the development of new products get out of hand as happened with the Rolls-Royce RB 211 engine, or to allow existing products to under-perform because of insufficient review of their contribution to profit. One manufacturer examined his product line and found that three of the twelve items in his range provided 81 per cent of the total profit, while two products were losing 15 per cent of the profit. Further analysis of the situation showed that the sales force was spending too much time on the unprofitable items, and too little on the major profit earners. A shift of emphasis in the light of this information led to reduced selling and promotion for the weak products which then became profitable because costs were down, and sales volume remained static. The resources released by this were put into the profitable areas which then doubled their return.

Many product ranges grow in a haphazard way as new products are added. Elimination of unprofitable lines occurs less frequently. An engineering firm decided to rationalise its product line and found that 635 out of a total range of 875 items were unprofitable. As a result it cut out 592 of them and profits rose dramatically.

Every aspect of marketing needs careful scrutiny, and the mix, because of its flexibility, is one area which can be modified relatively easily. For example, a manufacturer with his own distribution network found that half the orders received by the firm were loss makers, while a small number of bulk orders received by the firm made most of the profit. Faced with this information the firm could have shifted its selling effort to the major profitable customers and dropped the small ones, or used a different distribution channel for small orders, or charged more for them. It tested the market with mail order and independent wholesalers to see if the small customer could be served profitably, and the results showed that profits could be increased by 28 per cent if wholesalers were used for low volume orders.

These examples illustrate the need for control. If an organisation is to run as efficiently as possible, it must have sufficient information on the performance of the goods and services it provides, and a clear idea of how it will react to that information. Inevitably, the effectiveness of the control function is influenced by the quality of the information and the budget against which performance is compared.

10.2 The Need for the Marketing Budget

The market plan is constrained by the budget, which imposes cost and revenue targets. At the strategic level the marketing budget links closely with the overall budget for the company. The process of setting the budget forces departments to communicate with each other and produce a coherent plan. The Marketing Department should estimate what the level of sales could be for varying allocation of resources to the marketing mix. If this sales volume is greater than the production capacity of the firm then resources can be switched away from marketing to production. There is no point in spending money obtaining sales if the firm cannot produce enough to meet the demand. Similarly, the Finance Department will have to estimate its cash requirements to finance the selling and production levels. A company that is short of funds and cannot easily borrow more, either because the cost of borrowing (rate of interest) is too high, or because it is already highly **geared** (heavily in debt), may not be able to support the marketing and production plans.

Once the broad budget which contains marketing overheads such as administrative salaries, and the cost of achieving them, has been settled, it can be broken down by product, region and function. This reflects the detailed plan for the Marketing Department and includes the level of promotion, type of distribution and sales force. The more comprehensive the budget is, the more useful it is as a yardstick for control.

The sales-volume budget is important because it sets objectives for production from which capacity and capital spending, purchasing of raw materials, labour requirements and stock control follow. The sales-value budget combines the sales volume and the price at which products sell. It provides an estimate of revenue and hence profitability. Use of break-even charts will show the minimum acceptable level of sales for a given margin of safety, and determine the viability of the whole organisation.

10.3 Problems Associated with the Marketing Budget

Setting the marketing budget is more difficult than one for production. In a production estimate, there is a clear link between the costs of inputs and the value of output. For a given output it is possible to calculate the volume of raw materials required, the number of man hours necessary and the machine utilisation. Of course, costs may change as prices of raw materials alter, new technology may lead to different materials and quantities being used and unforeseen events such as strikes and shortages may prevent the targets from being reached. An urgent order may mean that more overtime has to be worked and thus increase costs; but the reasons for the discrepancy between actual performance and targets are usually fairly clear. Poor product performance and high cost may indicate the need for better quality control and less material waste. The decision of a competitor to increase his work force so that he can raise output does not alter the capacity of existing firms, nor does a change in market conditions. However, the same is not true for the marketing side where the links between input and return are not so closely connected. In addition, the relationships are constantly changing. A competitor's decision to spend more on advertising may affect market share significantly, although if brand loyalty is strong the effect will be limited.

Much of the expenditure in marketing leads to uncertain results. A company researching into new products and testing market reaction cannot know how they will be accepted if they are launched, and the return may take a long time to show. Of course, market research will help to give a picture of the future, but changed conditions during the early stage of a product's life may radically alter its chances of success. On top of this, the reaction to new or existing products may be very different from the expected one either because tastes change, or the market uses the product in a different way from that intended. When the makers of Kleenex introduced paper handkerchiefs they were intended for women to remove make-up. Inevitably this market was relatively small. Subsequent research showed why sales were so much higher than anticipated and allowed the company to reposition its product.

Not all marketing expenditure leads to immediate results, or affects the sales of any particular product. Advertising of one brand may generate an increase in sales of another, or in allied products, or in other items in the firm's range. By enhancing the brand name there may be a long-term advantage for all the company's products and this can extend way into the future for ideas that have not even been thought of. A company with an image for reliability will find this an asset when launching new products, just as much as a means of increasing sales of existing ones. Product and market research are likely to yield results for the full life of the product which may last many years, yet the bulk of the cost may be incurred in the early stages. Returns are not related to any conventional one-year budgetary period. We saw in Chapter 7 that the best sites for bill-board advertising were occupied by companies that used them all the time. Advertising a new washing powder or brand of frozen food is rarely effective unless it is spread over a long period. Wide distribution is more easily achieved by firms whose products have a reputation for selling well. Early success for a product will make it more attractive to the trade, and expenditure in launching it can reduce the money necessary to carry it through the later stages.

Although developing the budget and allocating resources is not easy, this does not mean that the process should be ignored. Setting targets gives a structure to the plan, and ignoring this process means that the chances of profitable performance are slim. The targets may not be accurate but they are necessary to get the product off the ground. There is a danger that the complexities of the relationships could prevent any action at all. Setting out an intended course of action as a yardstick for progress with regular information on performance minimises the chance of lost opportunities, and prevents a poor sales record from continuing too long. However, it is always possible that increasing expenditure may turn a poor performance product into a best seller. The control information is the basis for decisions on the mix to be taken. These occur during the life of the product and reflect or anticipate the changing circumstances in the market. If there were not targets laid down it would be more difficult to make the right changes. For example, if sales are above the expected level and production is at maximum capacity, then a reduction in marketing expenditure or an increase in price might be called for. If there is spare capacity then production can be expanded to meet the new demand. Without control information these changes would not be indicated. Conversely a shortfall in demand may lead to a cut-back in production unless the costs of doing so are greater than the savings. Such a situation could arise if, for example, the firm incurred high fixed costs in its own distribution network.

10.4 Types of Budget

There is no single method of controlling the marketing function that covers every aspect. Resources can be allocated in broad categories such as market and product research, or expenditure on the mix. The former covers the product's design and physical performance, as well as gathering and analysing information on the market and its likely interest in the product. Target spending on the mix and test markets provide limits to the amount that can be used to support a product. The budget may give an indication of the priority the company attaches to different products or product lines by allocating resources in line with the company objectives. Alternatively, the budget may be based on individual product performance and its contribution to profits. By concentrating on profits, it encourages concern in that field and ensures that resources are allocated on a merit basis. The danger with this system is that it may overlook the needs of individual products because the highest profit earner may not require as many resources as a product which is still in the early stages of the life cycle. However, allocating funds purely on the needs of individual products ignores the profit contribution, so a balance must be struck between profit and need in the short and medium term.

10.5 The Allocation of Costs

It is not always easy to decide what represents a marketing cost. Is the cost of financing and maintaining stocks a production or a marketing cost? Assuming a demarcation has been agreed, some costs, such as a commission for the sales force, special offers and certain types of product promotion, can be directly allocated to individual outlets, products or ranges. However, many of the marketing costs are not divisible. The fixed overheads may include the distribution network run by the firm, the provision of comprehensive after-sales service, as well as the administrative costs of the marketing department and the salaries of the sales force. The way these costs are allocated can influence the apparent profitability of each product and a contribution cost approach can be used, as in production. However, this also has pitfalls in that carrying unprofitable items may be necessary to support the sales of the profitable lines. Often it is easier to allocate costs by function so that there is a budget for advertising, distribution or selling. Comparing expenditure by function with sales over a period of time produces trends which may indicate the course of action to be taken. Performance in these areas is then analysed in many ways; for example, by product, region, customer and outlet.

10.6 The Use of the Budget for Control

Once the budget is established and the figures are communicated to the relevant departments, the basis for control has been laid. The tactical objectives in terms of cost and sales volume provide a framework for operation. The value of the budget is dependent on the quality of information used in its preparation. If targets are unrealistically high, or low, the budget fulfils neither role of direction nor control. A **variance** is the difference between forecast or budget levels and what actually happens. Positive variances increase the profitability of the organisation and negative variances, usually denoted by figures in brackets, reduce profits. Thus a fall in market overhead represents a positive variance, while a reduction in the volume of goods sold is a negative one. Since external factors and relationships between them, over which the firm has no control, play such an important part in determining marketing performance it is unreasonable to expect what happens in the market place to fit predictions exactly. However, acceptable variances should be agreed in advance and results outside these levels can lead to further investigation. If expected annual sales for a firm are set at 500,000 units then a shortfall of 500 units may be acceptable but if sales were down by 10,000 units some corrective action might be called for.

Sales in excess of targets require just as much investigation as under-performance. As sales information reaches the firm it can be examined to see whether a new market is opening up, or an existing one growing. In either case there may be significant possibilities for expansion. A firm that is closely in touch with the market is in a much better position to take advantage of any new opportunities. Failure to react may mean valuable sales are lost to competitors. Equally, under-performance may merely reflect a general drop in the market as a result of adverse economic conditions. Thus the firm has to keep a check on its market share.

10.7 Control in Action

An engineering firm manufactures five products which are sold in four major regions. Annual sales are forecast at £600,000 spread evenly throughout the year. After three months sales have reached £160,000, £10,000 above the target. However, this total figure can cover up serious under-performance in certain areas, so further analysis is required to examine how each region is doing. One possible breakdown of the figures is by the four regions.

Sales by Region – £'000s.

Region	Forecast	Actual	Variance	Per cent variance from forecast
Midlands	55	66	+11	+20%
South Wales	25	28	+ 3	+12%
North East	40	30	(−10)	(−25%)
South East	30	36	+6	+20%
Totals	150	160	+10	+ 6.67%

These figures show that none of the four regions performed as expected and each one would be examined further to discover the reasons. For example, the market in the North East is 25 per cent below forecast. This could be broken down by sales areas within the region.

Sales by Area for North East region – £'000s

Area	Forecast	Actual	Variance	Per cent variance from forecast
A	10	9	(−1)	(−10%)
B	15	6	(−9)	(−40%)
C	6	6	0	0
D	9	9	0	0
Totals	40	30	(−10)	(−25%)

This information shows that there is something seriously wrong with Area B. The company could then look carefully at the sales in this area which could be broken down by product, customer, sales force, distribution system and promotion.

Product analysis may show that a particular item in the range is no longer selling well. It may be that the market for this item has fallen because it is not required, or it has been superseded by an improved product made by a competitor. If a large proportion of purchases in Area B is made up of this product then the under-performance is explained and the company may need to develop a replacement. Further analysis of the information relevant to the area narrows down the nature of the problem and provides the company with the factors that will determine future policy. Control used in this way enables management by exception to be applied where problem areas are isolated and dealt with.

Many of the factors influencing sales are beyond the company's control. A major buyer may have gone out of business, in which case the company needs to find new markets, or sales may have fallen because of a temporary fluctuation in demand. A general decline in the level of activity in the economy leads to a reduction in demand. A change in exchange rates alters the relative competitiveness of domestic and foreign manufacturers.

Market share is an important indication of the company's position with respect to its competitors. Successful sales performance compared with forecast levels may mask a change in the market. For example, if sales are up by 10 per cent but market share has fallen by 50 per cent the results are not very encouraging. From these two figures it is apparent that the market has grown considerably and the company has not taken full advantage of it. Similarly a decline in sales needs to be viewed against the movement in the industry as a whole and market share gives an indication of the general trend.

10.8 Conclusion

Control and review plays an important role in keeping a company in line with its objectives. It provides information for new decisions in the light of changed market conditions. It focuses attention on the need for profitable operation and efficient use of resources. In those industries where profit is not a major objective, e.g. the nationalised industries, it is the means of ensuring minimum costs and maximum performance. All enterprises have some target return on capital. The limits to the control function lie in the costs of gathering the information and the benefits accruing from it.

Work Section

A. Revision Questions

A1 What is the distinction between control and review?

A2 Why is a marketing budget necessary?

A3 What is included in the marketing budget?

A4 How does the marketing and research budget differ from that of production?

A5 How can current marketing expenditure influence sales in the long term?

A6 What types of marketing budget are there?

A7 Why might the cost of stocks be considered as a marketing or production item?

A8 Why can sales in excess of the budget present a problem?

A9 What is a variance?

A10 Suggest two ways of breaking down control information on the sales of a product.

B. Exercises/Case Studies

B1 The marketing budget for Gannet Ltd was set as follows:

Sales – 10,000 units @ £10 each		£100,000
Distribution	£ 5,000	
Advertising	£15,000	
Sales promotion	£ 3,500	
Sales personnel	£10,000	
Departmental expenses	£ 3,500	
		£37,000
		£63,000

At the end of the year the company found that sales volume was down by 10 per cent, distribution costs down by 5 per cent and departmental expenses up by 10 per cent.

a. Calculate the actual figures and present them with the budget, showing the variances.

b. What reasons can you suggest for the variances?

B2 The budgeted and actual sales volume figures for three sales regions are given in the table below. The prices of the products are: A: £5, B: £10, C: £20. Produce a table showing the variances in volume and value and comment on your results, suggesting possible action where necessary.

Sales volume in '000s of units

Region	Region 1		Region 2		Region 3	
Product	Budget	Actual	Budget	Actual	Budget	Actual
A	8	10	12	16	14	9
B	6	4	16	20	8	10
C	4	2	24	20	8	10

B3 An engineering firm manufactures three products, each controlled by its own product manager. Product C is considered by the marketing department to be an essential part of the product range offered by the firm, and it has been introduced recently against the advice of the managing director. The firm has a minimum profit target of 10 per cent of sales revenue for each product. Overheads of £30,000 are allocated between products on the basis of the sales revenue estimates provided by each product manager.

Product:	A	B	C
Sales revenue (estimate)	£24,000	£10,000	£6,000
Direct costs (estimate)	£ 2,000	£ 1,000	£1,500
Actual sales revenue	£35,000	£14,000	£6,000

  a. Calculate the expected profit, based on the sales estimates.
  b. What is the managing director's likely reaction?
  c. How would the managers defend their products?

B4 The managing director of a trade newspaper was concerned about rising costs in the advertising department. As a result, he set up a budget for the department and reviewed the performance a year later.

	Budget (£)	Actual (£)
Total advertising costs	33,000	48,500
Comprising: Salaries and commission	10,000	17,000
Car expenses	6,000	7,500
Exhibitions	2,000	4,000
Production costs	15,000	20,000

When he received the figures the managing director was horrified to see how costs had risen. He compared absolute and percentage variances. It was clear evidence of poor cost control, and he demanded to see the advertising manager so that he could explain himself.

The advertising manager was annoyed. He pointed out that the managing director had ignored the rise in revenue (Budget £130,000, Actual £160,000). The managing director had refused to alter the budgeted costs although he had demanded increased business; there had been a 15 per cent increase in wages; they had held a larger stand in the national trade fair against the advertising manager's advice, and costs were expected to be up by 50 per cent. Inflation over the past year had been 20 per cent which was bound to hit production costs.

a. Comment on this situation, using the figures to explain what has actually happened.

b. What changes in the budgeting system would you suggest?

C. Essay Questions

C1 How important is control and review to the marketing function?

C2 Explain how you would set up a marketing budget, showing how you would deal with any problems that might emerge.

C3 'Marketing budgets have no value because there is no control over the factors that influence results.' Is this true?

C4 'Sales volume has increased by 25 per cent for each of the last three years.' Is this conclusive evidence that marketing performance is satisfactory?

C5 At a sales meeting one of the brand managers stated, 'We have met or exceeded our brand targets for the last five years providing the largest contribution to company profits.' How should the sales director react?

Chapter 11

Marketing Case Studies

Objective: *To draw together the marketing area by applying the theory to practical situations. To demonstrate the inter-relationships between the various parts involved in marketing.*

Synopsis: *The chapter is split into four separate cases. Two represent real situations and two take imaginary companies. The Biro Swan case examines the marketing mix and its contribution to the launch of a new product. Having established a dominant position in the market, competitors react to this and the success of the imitator and the attacker is influenced by their approach to the mix. The launch of Polyveldt looks at the need to alter a company's approach to the market so that it can expand its market share. By employing wide-ranging market research and technical development, Clarks were able to design a product and build up a clear brand image in a market where none had existed before. United Custards is a broad ranging case based on an imaginary firm involved in the manufacture of powdered foods. The aim of this case is to bring together some of the numerate techniques used in marketing and analyse the findings. In considering the move into a new market, the firm has to compare the costs and revenues associated with each alternative. Once it has made the strategic decision it has to devise a mix that suits the product within the constraints of finance and the market. The last case was an examination paper. Although not entirely marketing in content, the case covers the problems of a company faced with international competition. The management have to decide on the best strategy to ensure sales are sufficient to enable economies of scale to occur. Pricing is an important decision because of its implications for sales volume and profit.*

Plan of the chapter:

11.1 Biro Swan Ltd

The ball-point pen was a well established product by the mid 1950s. In the UK the best-known major manufacturing companies were Biro Swan Ltd and Scroll Pens Ltd (both British companies), the French company Bic Pens Ltd and the American Scripto Pen Corporation. In 1956 Scripto purchased Scroll and in 1957 Bic bought a controlling share in Biro Swan, thus giving rise to two large competitive units. The latter take-over was particularly significant because Bic was already well established in France. It was the largest manufacturer of ball-point pens, with 80 per cent of France's 100m. unit market. Bic wanted to make its presence felt in the British market through its new acquisition, Biro Swan.

In 1957 the prime objective of Biro Swan was to gain a new segment of the British ball-point pen market. Its first task was to make a clear assessment of what was happening in the market at that time. Once this information was available it could then plan its campaign carefully as to what action it felt was necessary and how it might carry it out.

Some of the information from its market research findings is set out in the appendices. A number of factors were clear:
a. Bic/Biro Swan had the largest share of the existing market for ball-point pens.
b. The ball-point pen market was the major growth market in terms of both volume and value.
c. The market was well catered for in medium and high priced pens.
d. The manufacturing costs of ball-point pens had fallen significantly in the previous three years.

Biro Swan prepared forecasts from its experience and from the market research information available, for the total market (volume and value) and for the share of the market that it might expect to gain, bearing in mind the product lines available. It decided that the best way to achieve its objective was to introduce a low priced ball-point pen. Biro Swan was now faced with the task of creating the necessary interest in this area by bringing together the various elements in the marketing mix to ensure the success of the plan.

Twelve months after the takeover (August 1958), Biro Swan was ready to launch its new product range under the brand name 'Bic'. The range consisted of three models: the 'Bic Crystal (5p),[1] the 'Bic Clic' (7½p) and the 'Bic Coronet' (10½p). The first two could not be refilled and were disposable.

For this launch there were three important factors influencing the marketing mix:

---

[1] Decimal equivalents have been used in this case.

1. The 'newness' of the product and its fit with a new market, identified by market research.
2. The price had to be cheap to sell the product. A disposable ball-point pen had to be priced at a lower level than any others on the market.
3. An intensive sales policy was necessary to gain wide distribution and keep prices low. This entailed short distribution channels as far as possible. The full value of the lower prices was made available throughout the trade, and 'van salesmen' were instructed to grant a 'wholesale' discount to retailers ordering large quantities. The van salesmen took orders and supplied them immediately from stocks they carried with them. This had significant advantages over firms that took orders and delivered later.

In support of the pricing and sales policy Biro Swan used its existing knowledge of distribution channels in the trade. It introduced heavy consumer advertising both in local press and television, carefully emphasising the nature of the new product and its extremely low price.

Reviewing the situation in September 1959, twelve months after the launch, the 'shilling throw-away', as it became known, appeared to be proving very successful. Production had reached 53m. units per annum, out of a forecast total of 85m. for all types of ball-point pen. However, in the wake of the Biro Swan launch, Scripto had introduced a ball-point pen (the Scripto 'long-line') similar to the Bic range in price and quality. It had sold 5m. pens by September without any serious advertising. It had been a wise move by Scripto because it allowed it to enter the market without too much effort, and gave it time to think what it was going to do about cheaper pens in the long term. In addition it was able to review its standard product lines to see whether any adjustment was needed there.

Biro Swan was concerned because Scripto had always emphasised quality and price as its hallmark and yet it seemed to be attacking the cheap end of the market. The criteria for Scripto's selling policy had long been based on quality, availability, appearance and price. Two-thirds of its output was sold through wholesalers and the remainder was sold direct to retailers and chain stores. However, in order to maintain wholesaler loyalty, it had a policy of never undercutting wholesalers when they sold direct to retailers, nor allowing discounts for bulk purchases. The selling operation was backed by a modest advertising and promotion budget based on 15 per cent of total factory sales.

While Scripto's cheap line was making an initial impact on the market, the company decided that its main effort should be in its medium and high priced products. It emphasised this by improving its range, through larger ink cartridges and better quality. This gave it a competitive edge over similar Biro Swan models. To make serious inroads into the 'cheap' market Scripto decided to bring out a model that was better than the 'Bic Crystal'. By August 1959 Scripto had increased its production capacity and launched the 'Bobby' at the same price as the 'Bic Crystal' (5p). It had the advantage of a retractable point. A major advertising campaign on television and in local papers was set for September when the 'Bobby' reached the public. The launch was supported through its trained salesforce by Scripto's long-standing distribution chain from factory to wholesaler and retailer, or direct to certain retailers and chain stores. The company continued its policy of never undercutting the wholesaler, and based its appeal, as before, on quality, availability, appearance and price. This appeared a strong package to challenge the position of Biro Swan, and the threat to its initial break-through had come to stay.

Aware of the generally different selling and distribution techniques that existed between the two firms and confident that its early position in the cheap market could be maintained, Biro Swan's approach was to look more to the medium and long term, and set objectives which would hit Scripto hardest in this range. For this reason, in late August 1959, it launched its attack by announcing price cuts in all medium and high priced pens in the Biro range.

Care was taken to safeguard wholesalers and retailers who held large stocks, and special offers were made to allow them bonus facilities if they acted on the price change quickly. It was reputed that such price cuts were to be supported by a £250,000 advertising campaign.

Appendices

Appendix I (Figures in millions)
Trends in the total unit sales of pens (UK)

	Ball-point	Steel nib fountain pen	Gold nib fountain pen
1952	11	4	1
1953	14	3	1¼
1954	16	3	1¼
1955	29	4¾	2
1956	38	6	2¼
1957	48	6½	2

Appendix II (Figures in £ sterling)
Trends in the total sale of pens (UK)

	Ball-point	Ball-point refills	Gold nib fountain pen
1952	900,000	1,100,000	1,200,000
1953	1,200,000	1,000,000	1,200,000
1954	1,300,000	1,100,000	1,300,000
1955	1,800,000	1,200,000	1,500,000
1956	2,000,000	1,000,000	1,400,000
1957	2,200,000	900,000	1,300,000

Appendix III (Market Share)
1957.   Market share was as follows:

Biro Swan	45%
Scripto- Scroll	22%
Others	33%

Appendix IV – Average factory price for ball-point pens

	In new pence
1952	8½
1953	8
1954	9
1955	6
1956	5
1957	4½
1958	4 (est.)
1959	3½(est.)

Appendix V – Estimated sale of ball-point pens

	Volume	*Value* (£)
1958	61m.	2,500,000
1959	85m.	3,600,000

(*Source*: Appendix I– V, Board of Trade)

Appendix VI – Product lines available (1957)

Biro Swan		*Scripto*	
Biro Line		*Scripto Line*	
Medium price	(Retail)	*Medium price*	(Retail)
Minor	15p	'250'	12½p
Citizen	19p	'490'	23½p
Retractable	22½p	'T200'	31½p
Stylist	29p	*High price*	
High price		'T6 50'	37½p
Delux	52½p	Satellite	85p
Squire	87½p	*Scroll Line*	
Magnum	95p	*Medium price*	
		'320'	17p
		'420'	19½p
		'520'	28½p

Questions

1. What was Biro Swan's short-term objective after being taken over by Bic?
   What factors contributed to it achieving this objective?

2. How was the mix used to support the strategy chosen by Biro Swan?
3. What were Scripto's main marketing objectives in retaliating against Biro Swan? To what extent do you think they were realistic?
4. Examine Biro Swan's medium and long term objectives and assess its value in fending off Scripto's challenge.

11.2 Clarks and the launch of Polyveldt[1]

C. & J. Clark Ltd has been producing shoes in Somerset since 1825 and it is now one of the largest shoe manufacturers in Europe. In 1970 it was essentially a product orientated company with a sizeable share of the children's market. It had become famous through its emphasis on 'care and concern' for feet which was reflected in the wide range of fittings offered, and the trouble taken in choosing the correct sized shoe at the retail outlets.

UK market share in 1970
Children's shoes	20%
Women's shoes	7%
Men's shoes	2%

Clark's marketing strategy was geared to mothers, who usually bought shoes for their children. Market research indicated that the priorities for parents looking for children's shoes were:

1. *Brand*:   Clarks had a clear advantage here because of its range of shoe widths. The disadvantage of many fittings is in the size of stocks retailers must hold. However because parents accepted the benefits of well-fitting shoes for their children, retailers achieved a reasonable stock-turn.

2. *Shop*:   Clarks shoes are sold through its own outlets and through other multiple and independent shops where trained staff advise about fittings and ensure that the customer receives the shoe exactly suited to the foot.

3. *Product*:   On the whole the consumer appeared to be relatively unconcerned with the design of the shoe, provided it was comfortable. Thus the appearance of the product was not too important, and Clarks continued to use classic, well-tried styles.

Whilst marketing strategy based on this order of priorities worked well for children's shoes (although design and appearance were to become more impor-

---

[1] With acknowledgements to Mike Greenwood, Brand Manager, Men's Shoes, Clarks, Ltd.

tant in the 1970s) it was not suitable for the men's market. Research showed that the order of priorities was reversed for men, with the product being the most important factor. The men's shoe market was not very fashion conscious and the styles bought were mainly conventional. As a result of this, there were no clear distinctive features between competitors' products, and men bought at the first convenient store which displayed the style they wanted, regardless of the manufacturer. There was little variation within the categories of casual (usually suede finish or desert boots) and formal shoes. Although Clarks had pioneered the desert boot in 1942, it faced increasing competition from similar looking but cheaper priced, lower quality imports. Since style, rather than the brand or quality, was the most important factor to the consumer, Clarks was bound to lose out.

Given the dominance of the children's market, most Clarks outlets were geared to women and children, and the men's range was more of an addition than a main part of the store. Many of the shops were in off-high street sites and so failed to provide the convenience men required. With product similarity an obvious men's shoe shop was more attractive to the market than the desire to buy any particular brand. Thus the Clarks strategy did not apply to the men's market, and this accounted, in part, for its low share of it.

In 1974, in America, independent market research into 'life styles' and how they were changing provided Clarks with the opportunity to create the distinctiveness it needed to build into the men's division. There had been a significant change in the workplace and at home. Women were working more, and the emphasis on menswear was increasingly in the casual/sports area. Taken with the fact that it was no longer essential for men to wear suits to work, the formality of shoe design could be relaxed. There had been considerable growth in the male toiletries market with deodorants, after-shaves and 'splash-on' colognes. Thus the picture that emerged was of lifestyles that emphasised casualness and comfort, and a wish to express more individuality. The growth of concern over health and the development of sports like squash, golf and jogging gave a major boost to the sportswear and associated leisure markets. This spilled over into the market for everyday clothing. As 'unisex' styles developed, so men were prepared to be more adventurous in their clothing and shoes. Formality was clearly 'out' except for certain occasions and levels.

Undoubtedly the general economic climate accelerated this trend. With declining purchasing power from wages as a result of inflation and unemployment, one area for cutting costs was in clothing. In 1975/76 there was a 40 per cent decline in the sale of suits in the UK market and an increase in the sales of jeans. In 1976 sales of jeans and slacks took 45 per cent of the market with 61.8m. pairs at a value of £254m. Increasingly men were buying sports jackets and trousers rather than suits for work, giving flexibility and individuality in what they wore.

In 1975, 52 per cent of Clarks sales of men's shoes in the UK were in formal designs.

Clarks Sales in the UK, 1974

	Market share	Sales
Formal	70%	485,000 pairs
Desert boots	30%	212,000 pairs

However, it had the technology and the mass production capability for the casual market. Although in England it was under pressure from competitors overseas – in Italy, for example – Clarks had a prestige image for its desert boots and overall manufacture for international markets meant that approximately 50 per cent of its total output was of casual shoes. Change was needed: Clarks was faced with competition against which it showed up badly in terms of the price of its product and the type of outlet through which its shoes could be bought.

From this situation the men's division developed the idea of the 'funny shoe' which came to fruition in the Polyveldt range. By the standards of the time, the design was extraordinary but it fulfilled the basic criteria for a successful product. Firstly, it was distinctive. Both the design and the construction could be protected by patent. Secondly, the durability of the materials gave it a strong appeal to the market; and thirdly, it fitted the general change in the clothing market by providing comfort, a casual look and something that was visually out of the ordinary. The shoe design had the added advantage that its flexibility meant only one width fitting was necessary for each size. This enabled economies to be made in distribution, allowing lower stock levels to be held by the retailer. However, consumer tests and retailer reaction were negative because of the shoes' appearance, and there was a reluctance in the trade to take them. Thus, if it was to be successful, the men's division had to force the shoe on to the market to show that it would sell.

Initially the North East was used as a test market. Retailers were persuaded to stock the product by being offered sale-or-return terms, something Clarks had not previously used. Display material was provided to support the launch. Promotion was designed to emphasise the characteristics of the shoe which would be favourable to the market, stressing comfort, durability, value and individuality. The market was told about the product directly through advertising and not primarily through the outlets because they did not have the pull on male shopping. The idea of a 'funny shoe' was new to the market and there needed to be a considerable amount of text explaining what the shoe had to offer, but the overall appearance of the shoe was played down. The first advertisements showed the soles of two shoes, one new and the other used with the caption, 'the pair on the right has walked 1,000 miles'. Once the reader's attention had been gained, the text sold the shoe. Advertisements were placed in publications which were read at leisure times. Double-page spreads were taken in the Sunday colour supplements and in the *TV Times* where the impact was likely to be greatest since they tended to remain around for a week.

Following the success of the test launch, Polyveldts were marketed nationally. With advertising used to increase product awareness, the market grew rapidly and temporary shortages developed. Technical problems in the manufacture of the sole led to premature cracking in some of the early shoes but customer loyalty was maintained by the quick replacement of faulty pairs. Once the problems had been overcome, Clarks began to make a sizeable inroad into the casual shoe market.

At this time there was a significant growth in the American market for 'earth shoes', as they were called. They were designed to assist posture and moulded around the foot, with a heel lower than the sole. The English market wanted more in the way of comfort and so Clarks introduced the 'Nature Trek' shoe nine months after the launch of Polyveldts. Using the same techniques as the Polyveldt manufacture, the Nature Trek went a stage further, encasing the foot in a supple bag of leather cut in a single piece. Advertising copy emphasised the structure of the shoe and the way it was moulded around the foot. The shoes and copy contained the Leonardo drawing as a 'motif', accentuating the naturalness and authenticity of the shoe. Like the original Polyveldt, it still looked unusual with a distinctive asymmetric seam. Where it was taken up as a cult it became known as the Cornish pasty. A smarter, more conservative design, 'Town Trek', was introduced to capture the comfort-based, semi-formal market. The natural culmination to this came in 1979 with the 'Side-stitch' which was a conventional looking shoe although using the Polyveldt type sole – formal appearance manufactured in non-formal technology. Again, Clarks used technology with promotional backing to provide consumer benefits – comfort, lightness, flexibility and durability.

By 1979 Clarks brand share of the men's market had almost doubled from its 1974 level and the brand is now the dominant premium casual brand in Britain.

Clark's share of the UK men's market

	1973	1974	1975	1976	1977	1978	1979
%	2.2	3.0	4.2	3.9	5.0	5.1	5.1

The Polyveldt product had developed in such a way that it virtually became the brand name. Advertising and promotion had been designed to make the market product-conscious and encourage customers to ask specifically for Polyveldt shoes. Initially it did not matter that the brand was not closely connected in the consumer's mind with Clarks, although advertising always linked the two.

Within five years Clarks became known as innovators using technology to develop distinctive shoes in both casual and semi-formal markets.

Questions

1. What were the main strands of the marketing policy of Clarks before 1970? In what way did the essentials have to change for the growth of the men's division to occur?

2. What research was undertaken before the launch of the Polyveldt shoes and how did its findings influence the policies of Clarks?
3. How did Clarks seek to obtain trade co-operation for the new product? What advantages were there for retailers?
4. What can you say about the marketing 'mix' as a whole and the way the different parts were inter-related?
5. How did Clarks develop extension strategies for the product and what future course of action could it take?

11.3 United Custards

United Custards Ltd manufactures a wide range of powdered foods which are sold direct to major buyers. Last year it found that sales of its product had fallen. There had been considerable inflation, and Government policies to cure it had led to a general reduction in the average income. At the same time, because of the drop in incomes more people were seeking employment and although the unemployment figures were rising more jobs were being taken.

Particularly hard hit by these changes were those service industries that could not absorb some of the cost increases through higher productivity. Some had virtually guaranteed markets, but others faced a considerable drop in demand as a result of lower incomes earned by their consumers.

The figures for sales last year were:

Customer	Tonnes
Cafés	75
Hotels	32
Schools	44
Office canteens	49

The company had raised prices by an average of £98 per tonne to £1,498 per tonne and sales had fallen from 220 tonnes per year. These figures worried the managing director since the company's capacity for powdered foods was 250 tonnes per year. Direct costs were £1,000 per tonne.

The marketing director suggested two possible courses of action:
1. The company could cut prices and bring production up to 250 tonnes in response to the increased demand. Research showed that over the required price change the price elasticity of demand would be the same numerically as for the increase in price last year. Output would have to rise to the full capacity.
2. The full spare capacity could be taken up by entering the domestic market, selling dried soups through supermarkets and independent retailers. Supermarkets buy direct from the manufacturer through their own buying offices. Independent retailers buy from wholesalers. The product range would be packet soups in a variety of flavours. Like existing competitors' soup packets, the weight would be 50g.

If this idea went ahead, the packs would be sold into the distribution trade at 16p each. Costs per pack would be as follows:

Ingredients	8p
Direct manufacturing costs	2p
Packaging	1p
Overheads	2p
Advertising	1p
Profit	2p
	16p

The marketing director is concerned about this price because he wants to achieve a reasonable market share. He is afraid that it may be difficult to sell into the trade because there is no established brand image. If the plan is adopted, and full market potential is reached, there will be a chance of an extension strategy with an 'instant-mix' soup which is already being marketed by a competitor. As yet the flavour of this kind of soup is unsatisfactory but the product research department feel that they will have solved this problem within a year.

The firm still has to decide on the branding of the soup range and how it will promote it. The managing director agrees to try moving into this market provided that he can be 89 per cent certain that there is at least a 20 per cent userhip of dried soups in the market. To discover this information, a quota sample of 5,000 people is carried out.

Additional market research findings are included in the appendix.

Appendix

Information on the dried soup market provided by a market research agency.

1. Per cent of users of dried soups by socio-economic
   group

A, B, C$_1$	40%
C$_2$, D, E	60%

2. Per cent sales by outlets

Supermarkets	65%
Independent retailers	35%

3. Per cent of users of dried soup

Single people	30%
Married with no children	10%
Families	60%

4. Existing margins
   Supermarkets   20%
   Wholesalers   5%
   Retailers   15%

5. Price of existing brands   Market share
   Own-Brands   17p   30%
   Brand X   19p   35%
   Brand Y   24p   25%
   Others   20p   10%

6. Attributes of soup important to consumers in order of priority:
   Flavour
   Nutritional value
   Consistency/texture
   Ease and speed of making
   Colour

In addition, you are given the following information:
For normal model with parameters n, p, q, the mean is given by n.p. and the standard deviation by $\sqrt{n.p.q}$.
The following table gives areas under a normal curve in standard deviation from the mean:

Standard deviations:	0.25	0.5	0.75	1.0	1.25	1.5	1.75
Area:	0.1	0.19	0.27	0.34	0.39	0.43	0.46

Questions

1. Explain fully the meanings of the three underlined terms (pp 170, 171).
2. What effect do you think inflation and government policies will have on United Custards' existing market, and why?
3. What is the price elasticity of demand shown by the drop in sales last year? Show your working. Do you see any problem in using average figures?
4. Given that overheads remain constant, is it more profitable to reduce prices and increase sales to the existing market, or leave them at the current level? Explain your answer. (It may help to look at contributions.)
5. On the basis of the information in the case, how many dried soup users are necessary from the sample of 5,000 people to convince the managing director that it is worth going ahead with the second scheme?
6. Draw the distribution channel for the soup market.
7. To the nearest ½p what will be the soup's final price to the consumer? How does the distribution system affect the manufacturer's flexibility in changing prices?
8. Should United Custards brand its soups?

9. Given the cost figures in the case, has the company any chance of reducing the price of the soup to help with the launch and still make sufficient profit?
10. How much money is available for advertising and how would you develop an advertising strategy for the soup? Give reasons for your answer.

11.4 'All the Talents' Clothing Ltd

'All the Talents' Clothing Ltd (ATT), based in an industrial town in the North West of England, manufactures shirts for all the UK market. It buys material from home and overseas suppliers, cutting, assembling and packaging the garments in its own recently enlarged factory. The product is at the top end of the market, having a reputation for good quality emphasised in occasional advertising. Most of the sales are through department stores and multiple tailors; ATT normally waits until approached by its buyers, although it has recently employed a salesman, who concentrates on independent retailers. The shirts are normally sold to shops at a discount of 50 per cent on recommended retail price; this, together with the good reputation of the company's product, has made it possible to insist on a fairly tight credit policy. ATT success-fully maintained sales of some 100,000 shirts for several years, although its profits have been disappointing lately.

The UK shirt market has grown slightly faster than real national income, although with fluctuations reflecting the economic cycle. However, the 'top end' has been stagnant for some years; the remainder, although faster-growing, is more competitive, with an increasing market share going to Asian and Eastern European products. A recent market research survey, commissioned privately by ATT, shows that there are three sections of the market as follows:

Shirt price	Annual sales	Imports as per cent of sales	Distribution channels	
£8–£10	10 million	5%	Department stores	40%
			Multiple tailors	50%
			Other	10%
£5–£7	40 million	30%	Multiple tailors	10%
			'Quality' multiples	50%
			Independent retailers	30%
			Other	10%
£2–£3	150 million	80%	Supermarkets	40%
			Variety chain stores	40%
			Other	20%

'There are too many imports – what we need is a good dose of *economic nationalism*,' says Mr George, the company's owner and managing director. Certainly ATT's profits have declined since 1975, although the board are not agreed as to why.

ATT's marketing director, Mr Fox, has been arguing for some time that the company needs to switch into the middle sector of the market. Recent figures for the industry suggest that sales for the product are very responsive to price changes, with a *price elasticity of demand of around 4*; this figure was given exact confirmation last year when the company cut the price of one line by 5 per cent and received a 20 per cent increase in orders. Mr Fox wants the recommended retail price of the company's product cut from the present £10 to an average of £7, and has calculated that profits will increase even without any change in marketing strategy (there is a profits forecast based on a retail price of £10 in Appendix A). Subsequent changes in the 'marketing mix' should add further to sales and thus to profits, he suggests.

There is certainly room for an increase in output. ATT recently spent £⅓m. on a custom-built production line, which with a second shift could produce more than double the present level of sales. If a normal week is worked throughout the year, capacity is about 120,000 shirts annually; overtime throughout the year could add another 40,000; and beyond this, a second shift would add at least 100,000. The likely *variable cost* in 1978/79 rises with each successive set of shirts, however:

Shirts	First 120,000	Next 40,000	Last 100,000
Materials cost each	60p	60p	60p
Labour cost each	75p	100p	120p
Repair and overhaul cost each	15p	15p	20p

The poor profit figures for the year just ended had been a particular disappointment to Mr George, as they fell far short of his forecast figure. He had been hoping for some recovery in profit margins after the decline in earlier years.

Year to 31st March	1974	1975	1976	1977
Sales	£320,000	£370,000	£395,000	£421,000
Profits (before tax)	£40,000	£45,000	£35,000	£29,000

In April 1977 he had drawn up privately a detailed forecast for the new financial year, showing prospective profits almost doubled. He selected what he felt the key figures – average shirt price, and total direct costs – and passed these on as targets to the marketing and production directors respectively. At the end of the year each reported proudly that he had met his target: but when the newly appointed chief accountant worked out the profits they were well short of the target. Sales were less than expected, and unit costs were up, as follows:

	Actual figures for 1976/77	Mr. George's forecast for 1977/78	Actual figures for 1977/78
Retail price of shirts	£8.60	£8.80	£9.00
Revenue per shirt	£4.30	£4.40	£4.50
Number of shirts sold	98,000	110,000	103,000
TOTAL REVENUE	£421,400	£484,000	£463,500
Direct costs per shirt			
Materials	45p	49p	55p
Labour	65p	69p	70p
Other	12p	12p	14p
	122p	130p	139p
TOTAL DIRECT COSTS	£119,560	£143,000	£143,170
CONTRIBUTION	£301,840	£341,000	£320,330
FIXED COSTS	£273,290	£285,000	£292,960
PRE-TAX PROFIT	£ 28,550	£ 56,000	£ 27,370

Annoyed and worried by this result, Mr George asked each director to comment on his department's performance (in the light of the recently revealed forecast). They replied as follows:

Mr Fox (*marketing*): 'We exceeded the target you set out, so I can't see what all the fuss is about. I'm surprised you expected the market to increase – things have been very difficult, and I told the production people twelve months ago that sales would be much the same. I suppose we could have cut price a bit, had we known what you were after.'

Mr Shelburne (*production*): 'We were spot on your target too, although I must admit that we couldn't have matched it at the production level you now say you wanted. I'd never have thought 130p a unit realistic – we knew all along that the materials cost would rise, and with sales below capacity we never had enough work to make optimum use of the labour.'

Mr Grenville (*administration*): 'I wasn't aware of any target for fixed costs, but in any case we couldn't have met your figure – interest costs and wage settlements were obviously going to push it higher.'

Mr George has now prepared a forecast of profits for this year (see Appendix A). He has discussed with the chief accountant ways of improving the company's chances of meeting this target.

ATT is a very long-established business, with a proud family tradition going back to 1806, but Mr George is the last in his line, and as the sole owner feels that he must take action now to decide its future after his retirement. He sees three possible courses of action: (a) to wind up the firm, (b) to find another company wishing to merge with his, or (c) to attempt to establish a workers' co-operative. The first will involve substantial redundancy payments, on the basis of one week's pay for each year's service – average service is about ten years, and the present wage bill is about £130,000. For the second, he has been advised that a purchaser would require a 10 per cent yield on its investment in the company. For the third, he would aim to sell to the workforce for the same price as in a merger, with them paying out of their savings over a period of years. The company's latest balance sheet is given in Appendix B.

Appendix A

Mr George's budget for the year to 31 March 1979 is as follows:

Revenue:	100,000 shirts at £5		£500,000
Costs:	materials	£60,000	
	direct labour	£75,000	
	other direct costs	£15,000	
	depreciation	£70,000	
	rent	£70,000	
	loan interest	£30,000	
	advertising	£20,000	
	administrative costs	£110,000	£450,000

Pre-tax profits	£50,000
Tax	£25,000
Post-tax profits	£25,000
Ordinary dividend	£15,000
Retained profits	£10,000

Appendix B

The latest balance sheet is as follows:

Shareholders Funds	£	*Fixed Assets*	£
Issued share capital	53,000	Plant and machinery	
Retained Profits and		(less accumulated	
other reserves	146,000	depreciation)	363,000
Long term Liabilities			
15% debenture repayable			
in 1988	200,000		
Current Liabilities		*Current Assets*	
Creditors	75,000	Stocks	79,000
Bank overdraft	27,000	Debtors	59,000
	501,000		501,000

Questions

1. Explain:
   (a) what *economic nationalism* is and how it would affect the company.
   (b) what assumptions are implicit in the statement that the *price elasticity of demand is around 4*.
   (c) why variable costs are higher if more shirts are produced.
   (d) how, given that the total cost of 100,000 shirts is expected to be £450,000 (Appendix A), the marketing director can argue for their sale to retailers at £3.50?
2. On the basis of Mr Fox's assumption about elasticity of demand, but ignoring any change in marketing strategy, calculate sales and hence profits for 1979 if the retail price is cut to £7.
3. Assuming that the change is made to the lower price, what changes in marketing strategy would you recommend?
4. As the newly appointed chief accountant, write a concise report to the board explaining as clearly as possible
   (a) why the company's profits for 1977/78 were £28,630 less than forecast;
   (b) what changes you would make to the whole budgeting system to make it more effective.
5. Explain how, as a skilled worker with 20 years' service with the company, you would view the three possible courses of action.

(Cambridge Local Examinations Syndicate, 1978. 3)

Glossary

Agent: A middleman who does not take *title* to the goods but acts on behalf of the buyer or the seller and expedites the transaction.

Audit: A continuous measurement of level of activity, used for market research, e.g. retail audit where regular checks on stock levels give an indication of sales over a period of time.

Brand substitution: See *Substitution*.

Budget: A detailed quantitative plan prepared within a business to cover a forthcoming period, e.g. profit budget, cash budget, sales budget.

Commission: A percentage of the total value of a transaction or a flat-rate fee earned in return for a service provided, e.g. commission retained by an advertising agency when paying the media on behalf of the advertiser.

Consumer profile: A picture of the consumer reflecting the characteristics of the market, produced by market research.

Convenience good: An inexpensive good that is purchased frequently, has several close substitutes and is easily available.

Copy: The text of an advertisement.

Correlation analysis: Technique used in forcasting which uses an observed relationship between two variables where one precedes the other in time.

Costs: 1. *Direct costs*. Those costs which are directly associated with the production of a product.

2. *Fixed overheads*. Those costs within a firm which do not change with changes in output in the short-run.

Cyclical variations: See *Variations*.

Demand: 1. *Effective demand*. Demand backed by ability to pay.

2. *Potential demand*. Demand when there is the ability to pay but where it has not been aroused.

3. *Latent demand*. Demand for goods not backed by the ability to pay.

Direct costs: See *Costs*.

Discounted Cash Flow (DCF): System for comparing alternative investment projects whereby future cash flows are given a present value by discounting them to the present. The extent of this discounting will reflect the *opportunity cost* of employing money in each project.

Display advertising: Advertising in the press other than classified or recruitment advertising.

Distinctive Competence: A particular strength of a manufacturer which can form the basis for product development and diversification.

Economic Man: The ideal fully informed and rational man who is self-interested and financially motivated. His decisions always optimise his economic advantage.

Economies of Scale: The advantages accruing to a firm which arise from falling costs as scale and specialisation increase.

Effective demand: See *Demand*.

Elasticity: Elasticity is a measure of the responsiveness of one variable to change in another, e.g. price elasticity of demand measures the responsiveness of demand to a change in price.

Factors of Production: Resources – land, labour, capital, managerial ability – used in the production of goods and services.

Fixed Overheads: See *Costs*.

Gearing: The extent to which a company uses other people's money and other people's assets to conduct its business.

Latent Demand: See *Demand*.

Market Potential: The performance the firm ought to achieve in the market given its present resources.

Market Share: The proportion of the total sales in a market gained by a firm or group of firms.

Marketing Mix: The combination of mix factors put together by a firm to market its products, e.g. distribution, advertising, sales policy and sales promotion, pricing.

Mean: The average of a series of data calculated by adding every item and dividing by the number of items.

Median: The middle item in a series of data when ranked in order of size.

Method of Moving Averages: A method of averaging figures through time to obtain an underlying trend in which there is a regular form of *variation*.

'Me-Too' Product: A product that is an imitation of one already on the market.

Mode: The most frequently occurring item from a series of data.

Noise: Any type of interference within communication, whether in the relay of the original message or in the perception of it.

Operational Research: An approach to complex problems whose characteristic feature is the use of models.

Opportunity Cost: The revenue that might have been obtained by an alternative course of action but that has been forgone in favour of the chosen course.

Population: In statistics, all the data from which samples are taken.

Potential Demand: See *Demand*.

Price System: System whereby the *factors of production* are allocated by the forces of supply and demand.

Product Life Cycle: A representation of a product's progress through successive stages from development to decline.

Product Substitution: See *Substitution*.

Resale Price Maintenance: The control by the manufacturer of the prices of his products charged to the consumer supported by common law.

Seasonal Variation: See *Variation*.
Substitution: 1. *Brand substitution*. Substitution of purchases between different brands of the same product.
   2. *Product substitution*. Substitution of purchases between different types of product.
Test Market: A small market reflecting the characteristics of the full market where new products or marketing strategies can be tested to iron out problems prior to the full launch.
Title: The ownership of a product.
Trend: The underlying pattern of a series of figures over a significant time period.
Variance: The variation that takes place between planned or budgeted and actual performance.
Variations: 1. *Cyclical Variation*. A variation from the trend caused by movements of the cycle, e.g. the trade cycle.
   2. *Seasonal Variation*. A variation from the trend caused by seasonal factors.

Index

G indicates a glossary entry

Acknowledgements

We are grateful to the following for permission to reproduce copyright material:

Audit Bureau of Circulations for Fig. 7.4; AGB Home Audit and National Opinion Polls for Fig. 1.2; Cunningham Willsmer and Cook Ltd for Fig. 9.4, adapted from Willsmer, *Directing the Marketing Effort*, Pan Management Series; Granada Publishing Ltd for Fig. 7.1 from Smallbone, *The Practice of Marketing*; Haymarket Publishing Ltd for the adapted article 'Carving Up Calculators' by Simon Caulkin from *Management Today*, March 1977; IPA for Fig. 7.3; JICNARS for Figs. 4.1 and 7.5; Kraushar and Eassie Ltd. for Fig. 6.3; L'Institut pour l'Etude des Méthodes de Direction de l'Entreprise (IMEDE), Lausanne for articles from the case studies 'Scripto Pens Ltd' M-110 and 'Smith's Potato Crisps Ltd' M-212, Copyright 1959 and 1968 by IMEDE; Macmillan, London and Basingstoke, for Fig. 1.1 from Baker, *Marketing, An Introduction; Marketing Week* for Fig. 5.1; Shaw's Price List for the diagram on page 113; Unilever Educational Publications for the storyboard on page 114; University of Cambridge Local Examinations Syndicate for questions from past papers in Business Studies 'A' Level.